Love Beyond Pain

Walk and Run While Wounded

Faye Thomas Fulton

BK

ROYSTON
Publishing

BK Royston Publishing
P. O. Box 4321
Jeffersonville, IN 47131
502-802-5385
http://www.bkroystonpublishing.com
bkroystonpublishing@gmail.com

© Copyright – 2019

Cover Design: Gad of Elite Covers

ISBN-13: 978-1-946111-71-5

Printed in the United States of America

DEDICATED

-To: Lord Jesus and the Holy Spirit for in Him I live and move and have my being.

-To: My mom and dad Thomas & Odessa Venerable for bringing me into this world

-To: My eldest son Bobby (son of my laughter and sometimes my pain, but a brilliant mind indeed and a great father and husband. I love you greatly. I am so proud of you)

-To: My eldest daughter Portia (daughter of my image and the better part of me that is strong wherein life I was weak. You are my strength and a woman I admire)

-To: My youngest son Quinton (my heart, son of my feelings thoughts and emotions, but also my determination and tenacity. Awesome talented like me) I love you son always remember that.

-To: My youngest daughter Jennifer (daughter of my heartfelt love and so many misunderstandings that forced me to reckon with myself. You forced me to love when I felt you didn't deserve it; but isn't that like God. Christ loved us even when we didn't deserve it. God's grace is shown through you my dear. I love you)

-**To:** All my grandchildren and great-grandchildren (I hope one day you will read this book and live, love, and laugh beyond life's pains for they will surely come).

-**To:** Cathy, Leslie, Ronnie, and Dina though you are my nieces you've loved me more like a sister. I am so grateful and thankful you're in my life. Don't ever stop loving me, I need you more than you will ever know.

-**To:** My precious and dear sister Ann Marie Adams Peyton. You caught me at a time in my life when I was dying and falling headlong into the abyss of life. You loved me unconditionally and without judgment. I trust you with my life. Over these 3 1/2 years, you've proven to be a faithful loving and supportive friend. No amount of words can be expressed from my heart what you mean to me my dear sister.

-To: your husband Ron, thank you for your love and friendship and considering me as your daughter!

TABLE OF CONTENTS

INTRODUCTION

Love must deliver. Love acts, and for every action there is a reaction. In Genesis 4:1 says, Adam made love to his wife Eve, and she became pregnant and gave birth to Cain. She said, "With the help of the Lord I have brought forth a man (NIV)." The pain of sharing your soul in what you think is love, can be like playing Russian Roulette. True love has a true target and accomplishes its aim or goal. The pain it takes to deliver love weighs heavily on the soul and body that carries it. Delivering love gives birth to new life in some instances. Cain didn't deliver in his act of love even though he was conceived in love. Adam and Eve had a child that hurt them to their souls. We all have sons' and daughters or loved ones that hurt us. Love was delivering as in the case of Jesus birth through Mary, with Joseph being her husband.

When we love beyond pains, our souls stop the abortion process of miscarriage before its time to deliver. We can miss the bigger picture or causes when we cannot see or understand the whys. Carrying a baby inside you 9 months is a long time. Can you imagine carrying a wound for 9 months in your soul? We cannot afford to carry soul wounds of rejection, mistreatment, misunderstandings, hate, or negativity. So, the greater question is how do we love beyond emotional pains to the soul? How do we fix what's broken inside us or dead? How do we recover from wounds that destroy us emotionally? How do we maintain and regain strength to avoid a soulish miscarriage that leads to spiritual death? Granted, somethings in your life need to die, but should you die with it? NO! Jesus had an answer. In his affliction on the cross as he laid bare wounded both mentally, and physically He asked the Father for a favor. Jesus said, "Father forgive them for they know not what they do." (KJV).

Jesus understood and considered not only their ignorance, but their weaknesses. He was able to become transformed, because he transcended into another state of mind. He elevated his broken body and wounded soul to a higher level of love within the Father's Spirit while in the flesh. Love don't hurt, people do. Why? Because of weaknesses and ignorance and because they are hurting souls too. When we can understand the human condition and frailties of weaknesses in us all, we can forgive and love beyond the pain others cause. We can ask for forgiveness when we are the offending party. I can love my children time after time again when they've injured me to the point that I want to die. For many years it baffled me as to why my kids continued to hurt me with words that cut me deeply. I tried to reason within myself and asked myself tough questions. "What have I done so bad and so wrong that my flesh and blood continue to hurt me?" Even at times when it was possible to have a talk I asked, "Is there anything I've done to you that's hurting you?" I've asked for forgiveness from my siblings. And I've asked for forgiveness from those closest to me the same.

We might not always know if we've hurt someone. But if it's brought to your attention, you should mostly certainly want to fix it. We are all weak and subject to human weaknesses that is why we need a power greater than ourselves. A love that supersedes our finite understanding of what we define love to be. Our strength must come from the Spirit of God to overcome these weaknesses. Jesus said, Father forgive them for their weaknesses and ignorance for what they are doing. Loving beyond pain transcends us above the physical into the spiritual realm of reasoning for that which Christ died. It opens us up to an enlighten and revelation that we can walk and run while burden with pains to our souls as he did. It teaches us to complete the course of life set before us as Jesus finished his purpose. Understanding the persons closest to you are just as weak and ignorant at times as you are allowing for sensitivity.

Ignorance is defined as a lack of knowledge of information, and unawareness or unconsciousness about something or someone.

Those that crucified Jesus was ignorant, and those that knew him such as the disciples were weak and afraid. When you get this revelation the blows to your soul can possibly experience a less impact. You will be able to walk and run while you are wounded from these attacks of disappointments, lies, betrayals, false loves, rejections and allow true love and forgiveness to heal you. Jesus was able to come down off the cross and walk away, if he wanted to. However, an incomplete purpose is a dead one. Jesus fulfilled love's call so that we are reconciled back to the Father. Not trusting in human weaknesses and ignorance's but trusting that God will carry you through the darkest hours of your life. Trusting that his love never ever fails. Accept Jesus as our great example.

OVERVIEW

The purpose of this book is to:

- Help the reader understand and overcome wounds to the soul by discussing why they hurt love ones and why others hurt them emotionally?

- What is going beyond emotional pains and how is it accomplished?

- Why did Jesus overcome physical and emotional pains and what was his solution?

- How can the 5 love languages written by Gary Chapman can go far and above a greater love than just meeting one's natural needs?

- Warning to parents of adolescent and teens

- Examine the 5 types of physical wounds and how do they correlate with wounds to the soul?

- Who in our lives create and do more damage to our souls and why?

- Is it possible to walk in the same higher dimension of love as Jesus did?
- Why do men love differently than women and why is there a divide?
- How to love beyond emotional pains from those with mental illnesses that are closest to you?

We are but a vapor in a vast world of other vapors. We are born, we grow, we live and love, we die. Living life with emotional pain is no fun for anybody. When you're in pain your soul feels as though you want life to end right now. Loving beyond pains of hurt through rejection, and physical abuse takes faith and courage. There is an inner strength that renews us and provides revelation and enlightenment if we are open to it. That revelation is a new day is on the horizon despite the pains experienced. It's only doable when Christ is at the center of your life. You can pick-up and look-up once more through the heart of His love. This book does not seek to give pep-talks, but possibly a new insight to grow, to feel love and be loved at a time when it seems impossible. See yourself like a flower, it has a process by which it thrives and lives and flourishes. But if it falls to the ground and dies, possibly there's a seed buried within a seed that regrows. Loving beyond pain means growing. To grow pass the darkness that engulfs you. To move beyond what's hurting your soul by allowing the sunlight of God's word to be present. The pain may still exist, but it does not define or dictate your next relationship or destiny. It does not constantly interrupt your life or distract your steps. It just means, you are aware of it. You give it no power to rule over your future. We are born to receive love, but we must watch whose definition of love we are embracing. The truth about love if you're looking for it, can be found in 1 Corinthians 13. If what you believe love to be doesn't line up with this, it's not love, it's dark love or false love.

What Doeth It Profit You?

Mark 8:36-38 King James Version (KJV)

36 For what shall it profit a man, if he shall gain the whole world, and lose his own soul?

37 Or what shall a man give in exchange for his soul?

There are a few key words within the scripture we must focus on so, the readers of this book will target their own soul first. Keep these words in mind. None of us are perfect, but we must examine our own hearts. When others have hurt our souls, what was your part in it? What did you give, gain, lose, or exchange?

Profit: to be of service or advantage or avail

Gain: to make progress, to establish a specific relationship

Lose: to miss from one's possession or from a customary or supposed place; to suffer deprivation

Give: to put into the possession of another for his or her use

Exchange: the act of giving or taking one thing in return for another; the act or process of substituting one thing for another; something offered, given, or received in an exchange

Commodity (Soul): the moral and emotional nature of human beings; the spiritual principle embodied in human beings

Every day, we all fall into one or two of these descriptions and quite possibly all of them. Our souls are the commodity or product that are the transaction. We profit or lose by our own **will,** which is part of the soul as we give it away "hearts" (soul) to something or someone, we gain something or someone or exchange it for something or someone. We risk being hurt to our souls because of our choices. Our treasures are spent-up in this world's affairs and this is the condition of the whole human race. The Bible talks about our souls a lot because it is there where the battle for our souls are fought. Your enemy cares nothing about your spirit because that belongs to God. Your body will go back to the earth from whence it came, but your soul's last destination is determined by your decisions.

LOVE

BEYOND

PAINS

Chapter One

God's Love or Emotional Love?

Let's try to define love a little bit before we begin so there's a slight blueprint of what a reader might think love is. We know that love can be defined in many ways and expressed in many forms; depending on whom we are loving. Love cannot be summed up in just one word, nor can it be defined as an emotion because it's not. Even the bible states, that love is of God (1 John 4:7). The word "OF" means, it comes from Him, it is sanctioned by Him. God is approving of love for He is love and not emotion. We can find many scriptures where love is described and defined and any time you see love in the bible, you should know it's God. It's funny how our definition of "love" can make us vulnerable to many different feelings that have nothing to do with love. Our understanding of love is more emotionally felt by separate degrees of loving depending on the relationships.

Applications and degrees of love are often used by an outline like the 5 love languages. The 5 love languages can be applicable to all of us as humans and they meet our human emotional needs. They are a necessary and vital part of life and being loved in the flesh as we know it and understand it.

Gary Chapman author of the 5 Love Languages denotes love as:

Words of Affirmation

Physical Touch

Acts of Service

Gifts & Giving

Quality Time

All can be summed up into love applications with varying degrees because we do not love everyone in the same way. Some appreciate being loved in one way, while others embrace it another way. By breaking down the varying relationships we then can see how a person's hurt and pain lead to some very crippling effects on the soul. Love is not an emotion, but we get emotionally through the acts of love. When Christ died on the cross, he took up His cross and suffered for sins once and forever for humanity. Sins he never committed. We too, must take up our personal crosses and die daily to them. These are acts of love played out, Why? Because unlike Jesus, we commit sins and continue to do so every day while in the flesh. Furthermore, taking up our cross and dying daily is signified by our constant crucifying of thoughts and actions of sin. Our spirits agree with the Holy Spirit, standing ready to guard against our souls which is our minds, intellect, will and emotions. Therefore, we are admonished to walk not after the flesh, but after the Spirit. The reality of this for most is we, spend 80 to 90 percent of our waking moments in the soulish realm.

James 1: 12-18 (KJV)

> [12] Blessed *is* the man who endures temptation; for when he has been approved, he will receive the crown of life which the Lord has promised to those who love Him. [13] Let no one say when he is tempted, "I am tempted by God"; for God cannot be tempted by evil, nor does He Himself tempt anyone. [14] But each one is tempted when he is drawn away by his own desires and enticed. [15] Then, when desire has conceived, it

gives birth to sin; and sin, when it is full-grown, brings forth death. [16] Do not be deceived, my beloved brethren. [17] Every good gift and every perfect gift is from above, and comes down from the Father of lights, with whom there is no variation or shadow of turning. [18] Of His own will He brought us forth by the word of truth, that we might be a kind of first fruits of His creatures. (KJV).

We are born with choices. You can choose not to allow negative or evil thoughts to enter your mind. This is our fight, our battle every single day. Life events are going to present itself if we continue to live. It's how we confront these events that determines our victory in our souls. You decide whether thoughts will be met with a YES, I WILL or NO, I WON'T. I'm the first to say that I do not protect or guard my heart every day, but I should. To suffer in the flesh means to cease from sin. Galatians 2:20, "I am crucified with Christ nevertheless I live: yet not I, but Christ liveth in me: and the life which I now live in the flesh I live by the faith of the Son of God, who loved me, and gave himself for me." (KJV).

True discipleship is all about living a daily life that mirrors Jesus. He is your mentor, for example, in all that is good. What did Jesus do in His daily life? Jesus was absolute, focused, determined, resolute in his divine purpose. Any time his flesh even wanted to go another way he said, "Not My will, but Yours, be done." Luke 22:42. He took up His cross every day to fight against the will of the flesh. He came to become acquainted with us. However, in all his earthly temptation, the Bible tells us he was without sin. In his flesh he knew no good things existed, so he was tempted on every side but never fell to commit or submit to sins. When the bible tells us to be transformed in the book of Corinthians, it is a process we are going through for sanctification. We are already justified through Christ, but now it is our responsibility to be cleansed daily. You wouldn't take a bath once a week, would you? You wouldn't brush your teeth once a week, would you? Well, as believers we also wouldn't renew and be transformed only once a week. It's a daily process, in order to love like Christ beyond our souls' inclinations. Every day you should be able to look in the mirror and see yourself being transformed from this sinful nature into becoming more like Christ. As a believer the fruit of the Spirit through the workings of the Holy Spirit should be evident to you first, then to those that know you "(family, friends), then your community, then to the world abroad. Yes, some will reject you, and not like the new you, but that's your opportunity to be a witness. You might get rejected, but that is the life of Christ. He came unto his own and they received him not. If your own rejects you for being transformed, that should tell you something is changing in you. "Not that I have already attained, or am already perfected; but I press on, that I may lay hold of that for which Christ Jesus has also laid hold of me." Philippians 3:12.

> "Therefore, since Christ suffered for us in the flesh, arm yourselves also with the same mind, for he who has suffered in the flesh has ceased from sin."1 Peter 4:1

To be spiritually connected with God, a divine higher power greater than self is through Christ that we obtain truth and revelation of what and who love truly is. God's laws of love (1 John 4:7,8). One can only forgive emotional pain by and through the workings of the Holy

Spirit. You cannot love without forgiveness and you cannot forgive without love. You cannot walk in the law of God's love without the Holy Spirit's guidance. Loving beyond emotional pain so you can live again requires a forgiving spirit and a heart of love. It takes forgiving yourself and the courage to rise up above the emotional impacts. Even as the Apostle Paul suffered for the calling placed on him to go unto the Gentiles with the message and mysteries of God, I too, have suffered greatly and for a very long time to bring you this message from God's heart, to mine, to yours.

People that hurt you might not ever ask for forgiveness, but that should never be a reason not to forgive them? The person could be dead and gone or moved to the other side of the universe. However, love, life and forgiving will be a part of your world by choice. Sometimes your expectations are just that, yours. My expectations out of all the hurt and emotional pains I've suffered in wanting love were just that, my expectations. Since those expectations belonged to me, I take ownership of how they will form and define my life. That is why it's important to have these vital discussions about love, relationships, and expectations. All feelings, thoughts, and emotions are within our own personal governing control. When we entrust these areas of our soul to another, we give them permission to leave an imprint within us. Oftentimes, that trust is broken, and we are left devastated through a series of events. Remember, just as you gave that permission, you have the power to resend it and move on. "IT' S NOT THE END OF THE WORLD" I use to think so, however. I chose to love beyond the pains inflicted on me by someone else. That person or persons do not dictate my responses or reactions. If it doesn't work out should I blame those parties for the rest of my life and die? NO! But each one is responsible for his or her share of hurt. Your family, friends, and many others are going to hurt you. You will hurt them too in some way or another. Our choice to hurt another stem from weaknesses and ignorance.

We are born with choices, but if you give those precious choices to someone else and they messed over them, then what? Yes, it's about power, the power to decide who or what governs your life's journey for the rest of your life. How to love beyond emotional pain, is about taking back who you were prior to giving your soul away. You entrusted your love, but someone destroyed it. Take note, love moves, it acts, it never stands still, and it never dies. To love, is to be human as they say. I say, to be hurt after loving is even more human. You owe it to yourself to be human and to still love despite what has been done. Forgiving someone is a powerful act, it requires dying to so many of your own personal thoughts, feelings and desires to exact revenge. It also requires, your soul to experience going through the process of inner healing. It requires love from the Holy Spirit to first comfort you, guide you, and lead you first to the truth of God's love. This is done so, that you may have the presence of mind to absorb and bounce back from emotional wounds.

The same love that kept Jesus on the cross, is the same love that lives within every believer that is filled with His Holy Spirit. This type of love is what I call 'SPIRIT-FILLED RESILIENCY' Spirit-filled as stated in Ephesians 5:17-21 says, "Therefore, do not be foolish, but understand what the will of the Lord is. Do not be drunken with wine wherein excess, but be filled with the

Spirit, speaking to one another in psalms and hymns and spiritual songs singing and making melody to the Lord with your heart, giving thanks always and for everything to God the Father in the name of our Lord Jesus Christ submitting to one another out of reverence for Christ" This scripture is making an inference and contrast by stating being filled with the Spirit is equivalent to being drunk with wine. Have you ever been drunk with wine or high off some other substances? You know what that feels like right? In addition, there are a few instructional keys included here. They are 1. Speaking to one another in psalms, hymns, and spiritual songs. 2. Singing and making melody to the Lord with your heart. 3. Giving thanks always and for everything. 4. Submitting to one another out of reverence for Christ.

Resiliency means, 'The CAPACITY TO RECOVER QUICKLY' from difficulties and tough times. To be able to spring back into shape. Having elasticity to recover back to the size and shape after deformation caused by compressive stress" (online dictionary) What are some ways we can begin that process of walking and running while wounded?

"Words of Affirmation" is one way we can speak positively to our souls. We can say, I am a forgiving and loving person. I chose to forgive all those that have hurt me. I acknowledge that I am, or I was in great pains to my soul I wanted to die. But I now affirm, that love resides within me. Greater is He that is in me, than he that is in this world. I acknowledge and affirm that I gave my whole heart willingly to be loved by someone I trusted. They broke that trust, but I also acknowledge, that I forgave him or her. I affirm and acknowledge, I will always love beyond my pains and my sorrows. I affirm and acknowledge, God would have me at peace with His gladness and joy. I am His delight and in Him I can put my trust.

What is the definition of *"Affirmation?" it's a positive declaration, a solemn oath, words of encouragement (Merriam-Webster, 2018)*. We know that the word of God affirms and acknowledges the people of God all through the bible. We selectively chose in times of defeat or victory which scriptures to use when affirming and acknowledging God's love for us and others. The following Psalm tell us the state in which our souls can become consumed. It also shares with us our longing for the laws of God's love when we feel low. Others arrogantly accuse us, and we feel that the truth will never see the light of day. However, the word of God has an answer and outlet for our wounded souls. The Lord will strengthen us in times of weariness. It's our responsibility to focus on His statues and love to remain accountable, teachable, as we remember who we are in Him. There are many souls' in your life that you'll encounter. If you live even to age 20 or 25, these vapors of souls will injure you in some way and for some reason. The price we pay to be human, is the price we pay to love one another.

WARNING FOR THE YOUNG AND INNOCENT

Teenagers and adolescent have a difficult time during their development. The guidance of parents is crucial to help them navigate through the soul vapors. The principles of God's laws of love apply to them as well. Parent's must teach them early the fruit of God's Spirit, as well as putting on the whole armor of God, especially in these days and times. Kids can be very cruel, and some can be dangerous. They cannot appreciate the affects of their behaviors. Parents need to step up to the plate and take more responsibility. Teach them respect towards others, teach them love and kindness and how to give and not always take. For this age group I encourage parents to keep their kids close. Don't allow someone else to wander in your garden of flowers, plucking them up at will. Watering them with values that are not approving of you as a believer. The bible tells us, the devil is a thief that comes to steal, kill, and destroy. He comes in liken unto a roaring Lion seeking who can devour. His order of the day is to rob you of the gifts God has entrusted to you. In the age of technology, we have placed our kids heads on the chopping block for the darkness of this age to consume their attention and minds and draw them away into foolishness. Young people have many more years to have their souls injured than those of us that have lived and bare the scars of life. Instead of teaching them about how to use their new phones and other electronics, teach them about the Holy Spirit, the Fruit of the Spirit, the Nine Gifts of God's Spirit, and the whole of God. These are spiritual defenses they will need to guard against all this perversion within technology. This is the best spiritual developmental gift you as a parent can give them. Warn them of the wickedness and darkness of rulers of darkness. This is not a scare tacked, it's the truth. My kids didn't encounter what the kids of today are experiencing, but it was still a battle. I have 11 grandchildren, and I thank God their parents have a foundation they can ground their kids on if the so chose to. If they don't woe unto to them as well. Being a believer for the youth of today is not popular, but this is not a contest, but a war and a battle for their souls. Teach them how to love beyond pains.

Psalms 119: 20-50

20 My soul is consumed with longing for your laws at all times

21 You rebuke the arrogant, who are accursed, those who stray from your commands.

22 Remove from me their scorn and contempt, for I keep your statutes.

23 Though rulers sit together and slander me, your servant will meditate on your decrees.

24 Your statutes are my delight; they are my counselors.

25 I am laid low in the dust; preserve my life according to your word.

26 I gave an account of my ways and you answered me; teach me your decrees.

27 Cause me to understand the way of your precepts, that I may meditate on your wonderful deeds.

28 My soul is weary with sorrow; strengthen me according to your word.

29 Keep me from deceitful ways; be gracious to me and teach me your law.

30 I have chosen the way of faithfulness; I have set my heart on your laws.

31 I hold fast to your statutes, LORD; do not let me be put to shame.

32 I run in the path of your commands, for you have broadened my understanding.

33 Teach me, LORD, the way of your decrees, that I may follow it to the end.

34 Give me understanding, so that I may keep your law and obey it with all my heart.

35 Direct me in the path of your commands, for there I find delight.

36 Turn my heart toward your statutes and not toward selfish gain.

37 Turn my eyes away from worthless things; preserve my life according to your word.

38 Fulfill your promise to your servant, so that you may be feared.

39 Take away the disgrace I dread, for your laws are good.

40 How I long for your precepts! In your

righteousness preserve my life.

41 May your unfailing love come to me, LORD, your

salvation, according to your promise;

42 then I can answer anyone who taunts me, for I

trust in your word.

43 Never take your word of truth from my mouth,

for I have put my hope in your laws.

44 I will always obey your law, for ever and ever.

45 I will walk about in freedom, for I have sought

out your precepts.

46 I will speak of your statutes before kings and will

not be put to shame,

47 for I delight in your commands because I love them.

48 I reach out for your commands, which I love, that I may meditate on your decrees.

49 Remember your word to your servant, for you have given me hope.

50My comfort in my suffering is this: Your promise preserves my life.

REFLECTION & NOTES

The word *"unconditional"* is used by some to gain leverage over another. This word controls those that are sometimes ignorant and weak. Unconditional means, "not subject to any conditions" but unconditional love means, that the act of that love is always not going to be easy or feel comfortable. Unconditional love should mean to always be truthful using the fruit of the Spirit through the workings of the Holy Spirit without judgment, prejudice or retaliation. Some use of these words is to decide whether the other person in the relationship will be devoted to him or her unconditionally to their agendas. It's a sad day when the power of loving someone unconditionally is weaponized in such a way as to control the other's behaviors. Affirming your love to someone should never be used in such a manner. Brain-washing techniques in any relationship should never be used. Words do matter when used to dictate or control one's emotions. *"Do you love me unconditionally?"* could have been used by Jesus asking Peter in John 21:15, Simon Peter, "do you love me more than these? Jesus asked this question 3 times. Not because he wanted to know if Peter loved him unconditionally, but to impress upon Peter's love for him in connection to others not so lovable. To love when it's not convenient. In His personal mission, Jesus already knew the minds of men. The question was for Peter's sake, not Jesus doubting it. Unconditional love by human definition can be taken out of context.

Peter was led to affirm and reaffirm the love he declared for Jesus. When someone affirms and reaffirms their love for you over time a great deal of trust is established. Everything begins with a WORD. I love you are vital important words to the souls longing "I Love You" Those three words have built nations and destroyed continents. Those words have mended hearts and killed families, healed broken relationships, and devastated marriages. There's something about someone affirming their love for you that's tightly woven and imprinted. How does anyone find the strength to recover from being broken and crushed to the soul? How to love beyond emotional pain and survive it is the question. Many have died literally of a broken heart from emotional stress. Some commit suicide, some have killed others. Some have attempted to kill, while others never love another again. It's a travesty when you give your soul over to another person (your mind, will, and emotions) and for whatever reason, he or she murderers it by default. When someone else's definition of love fails you, don't fail in loving yourself. True love never fails, as a believer your definition of love has a measuring stick. If you believe in Christ's teachings, then 1 Corinthians 13:4-8 is your love bar.

Are you rooted deep enough when emotional blows come to your door? The only way to recover hurt and pain is to forgive it stand-up and take a deep breath of faith to love again. Understand and gain the revelation that all of us are weak and ignorant. This is the condition of our humanism. That is why we are admonished to walk in the Spirit. We are told not to fulfill the lust of the flesh and of the mind. We think Jesus died for us with unconditional love, NOT TRUE. His love was very conditional. The conditions of his love were BELIEF, to believe that he died and bored our sins. The condition of his love was accepting him through salvation. Romans 10: 9. If thou shalt confess and believe in your heart the Lord Jesus thou shalt be saved, "conditional" The conditions were 'trust.' Trust that he loved you enough to die. Trust that he understood your weaknesses and your ignorance. It requires us to forgive others. It requires us to love our enemies and those that use, abuse and spitefully take advantage of us. It requires us to love beyond debilitating injuries to our soul, and sometimes body. Jesus soul was crushed, and His body beaten and bruised beyond recognition. The only thing He could do to get relief was to cry out from His soul. Father, please don't destroy them, but forgive them of their weaknesses, and the ignorance they do. Father, I have come and lived amongst them, and in their flesh is no good thing, so I crucify my flesh on this cross in their behalf. I will bear their sins and be bruised for their iniquities only you Father look passed them and see me as a ransom for their sins. Sometimes, our souls can become so heavy we cry out for God to take us from this world.

Many nights I begged and pleaded with the Lord to please take me from this earth. The times I laid on a couch for weeks I didn't eat or drink. I only got up to empty the fluids my body was producing for me to flush. I could feel myself dying, drifting away, wasting away. The emotional pains of hurt were so deep inside me no amount of prayer could recuse it. The shame of it all, who could I tell? where could I go? when would it all just be over? The loneliness was the hardest part of living. I was alone no matter my efforts to cry out to my sisters. The pains of being rejected by family can cuts deep into your soul too. But no matter who cuts your soul forgiveness and love must still be your foundation. Out of all the years of hurt, there came a time in my life wherein I hurt someone that loved me. Even though I asked for forgiveness and was forgiven, the guilt I felt of hurting someone else was unbearable. Deliberately hurting someone was not who I was as a person. Loving beyond pains also means forgiving yourself for the pains you've caused. Love yourself beyond what you've done is the order of business. On another occasion, I laid in bed literally for 4 months, and I ate very little. This self-inflicting wound landed me in the hospital near death with pulmonary embolism in both lungs.

I was rushed to the ER, doctors told me I should be dead. They said, "We only find these types of clots in the lungs after the autopsy." I wasn't loving beyond my pains of guilt and shame. There were no words of affirmation I could find within. No words of acknowledgments nothing. The greatest revelation you can possibly have, is knowing that Jesus loves you. He wants you to live for his glory. God knew, in His coming to earth in the form of man through Jesus the penalty for living was dying. He is acquainted with all our weaknesses, and ignorance. He fully knows living in this life presents hard challenges. If he didn't think we could overcome them through him, he wouldn't ever allowed us to exist. Imagine someone loving you so much that he or she is willing to leave their world of existence just to come and experience your world. God extended his mercy of love while we were yet sinners he died. God our Father left all of eternity and prepared Himself a body to be transformed from divine to human. He loves us just that much. He wanted to get to know us in an intimate and personal upfront way. WHAT A LOVE ACT!

The Lord loved us beyond His own pains and sufferings. He also knew that He would suffer a horrid beating and death, along with abandonment. Is it possible for any of us to 'Love Beyond Our Pains, So We Can Live Again?' YES, WE CAN! Love paid the price, but forgiveness was its currency. When you can look yourself in the mirror and openly and honestly say, "I FORGIVE ALL, SO THAT I CAN LOVE ALL," then you're living beyond pains. Pain is not dismissed because forgiving has occurred, let's be clear. Pain is pain. When you experience a cut to the body, you feel it no matter how superficial it might be. If it's a surface cut, it will take a few days or so to heal. If it's a deep tissue cut, it will take weeks and pain is still present. If it reached the muscle, it might take months. If the bone has been broken, it could be anywhere from 6 months to a year.

You can forgive and still feel the effects of pain. This is the walking and running while wounded process. Allow God to heal the pain just like a body wound will heal with time. However, more importantly, you affirm that you will still love and be loved despite the emotional pains. This is your victory over others and self-destruction. Don't use another relationship as an antidote, or to self-medicate. This is never fair to the new relationship. Courage, honesty, and being true to self and living in the higher level of love through faith is the key. It's normal after a dreadful experience for the body to go into protective mode. The brain sends these natural occurring signals to the nervous system to fight or flee. Our first reactions are to flee of course. Go hide from the world unable to face the awful truth that you've been hurt to the soul. You tell yourself, never ever will I allow anyone to touch me ever again. This is not loving beyond your pain, this is giving in to it. Shame is a part of the emotional feeling. Shame and embarrassment that you've been taken.

Forgiveness is not always a two-way street. We know many people die harboring unforgiveness, never letting go of the pain they felt. You don't have to be that person, you have a choice today to overcome it. It's easy to milk or nurse such wounds. It requires no big effort or strong will to do so. Your soul at times won't allow you to raise your spirit up above it all. Negative energy like hate takes more than giving a smile. Here is where the love and the mind of Christ must come in. The crucifying of the soul and the flesh is the battleground within. There is a preparation time through the washing of the word that must take place to drive those dark forces out of the mind. By yielding to the Holy Spirit you can survive your pains, but you can't do it alone. Humble yourself before a mighty God, ask for strength, and His love to guide you. It's your will, or His. When we release it to the Lord incredible insight and releases take place. God begins to reveal truth to your mind and insight to your soul. In my situations, I was able to regain enlightenment through my sufferings. The Spirit of the Lord took me back to the day of Jesus death. I was able to see the agony of his suffering. I was able to experience a higher dimension of love through his pain.

We are never taught to love ourselves, are we? Throughout life, we are taught to "love our neighbors as ourselves". More emphasis is placed on our neighbors then self. What if we turned that around and quote it another way? Love yourself, then as you love yourself, love your neighbors just as much. When we can love ourselves enough, we can then forgive the offending party. Love beyond pain, is about taking away from your own mind, soul, and body that which is hurting or killing you slowly. It's about the realization of the human condition with all of its weaknesses and the ignorant things we do. The fact that another person has injured you

29

emotionally won't change. Importantly, the fact also is true you don't love yourself good enough to heal from it. To keep a wound open is to invite infection to invade other parts of the body. In your emotional wounds, your soul is open. The invitation is no longer private, but open to public enemy number one. Attacks of diseases, other emotional traumas are invited to come along and have a party at your expense. You've heard the song "It's a Thin Line Between Love & Hate?" believe it or not, it really is. You have two choices in the matter, to love or to hate self. Another saying "Love Conquers All" whose and what love are you referring too? We have a poor concept of love. Take notice when we embrace what we think love is, it never works out.

The scriptures state, "For God so loved the world that He gave His only begotten son, that whosoever believe on Him shall not perish, but have everlasting life." (KJV) Let's look at this another way, for God so loved "Himself" himself being whatever He created. Everything God created He saw as good. He created us in His image; therefore, He loves Himself within us. He gave back to Himself, that which He so loved. We know that Jesus is God in fleshly form. He loved Himself so much He wanted to be closer to that which was a part of Him. Does that make sense? To love beyond your pains, you must see the good in all bad, and turn that which was meant for bad back to good. This is the reality of our existence. We acknowledge that bad was committed, but we deny it to rule over self. Affirm your love for self-first, and then you will be able to release the pain, so you can love others.

God being all knowing and, in all things, knew there was no good thing in our flesh. In Romans 7:18 says, "For I know in me (that is in my flesh) dwells no good thing: for to will is present with me; but how to perform that which is good I find not." (KJV) Since He knew within our design there was 'no good thing,' he also knew being born again takes you from the flesh into the spirit by becoming transformed. Romans 12 "I beseech you therefore, brethren, by the mercies of God, that ye present your bodies a living sacrifice, holy acceptable unto God, which is your REASONABLE service. And be not conformed to this world; but be ye transformed by the renewing of your mind, that ye may prove what is that good, and acceptable, and perfect, will of God." (KJV) A living sacrifice means we must crucify our flesh with all its deeds. If we walk in His Spirit, we will not fulfill the works of the flesh. This is where His love enables us to rise to a higher love beyond any emotional and physical pains we experience in this flesh.

REFLECTION & NOTES

Chapter Two

Love is an action word, and *physical touching* is an act. When we say, "I love you" this word at times seem to stand still in midair. The word of God says, "Dear children, let's not merely say that we love each other; let us show the truth by our actions. "(1 John 3:18, NLT). When our actions begin to speak louder than our words, a whole new level of love begins to take shape. When we experience emotional injured by a loved one, it hurts bad. That love bar has a closer relationship then a stranger. A wounded soul feels these emotional pains because the soulish and physicality of our humanist with another individual. Everything said, done, and inferred to the soul became a part of their DNA. In an article written by Sara from the Heart-Math Institute in 2013 on "Emotions can change your DNA" stated:

> "-It was not until the 19th century that substantial written empirical analyses of emotions began to emerge, when noteworthy figures such as Darwin and Freud took more scientific approaches. After being within the domain of philosophers for thousands of years, emotions are now closely scrutinized in 21st

century research laboratories, where scientists can observe their effects on human DNA" (2013) ***"Intention Shown to Be Potent Force"*** *In addition, she further included some fascinating findings from research that Heart-Math uncovered. Cell biologist Glen Rein and IHM Research Director Rollin McCraty conducted a series of experiments in the early 1990s involving DNA and intentionally generated emotions. A decade later interest in these experiments persisted. After numerous requests, McCraty summarized their data and published the results of the research in 2003 in a brief report titled Modulation of DNA Conformation by Heart-Focused Intention. "The results provide experimental evidence to support the hypothesis that aspects of the DNA molecule can be altered through intentionality," Rein and McCraty wrote. "To our knowledge, this study was the first to correlate specific electrophysiological modes with the ability to cause changes in a biological target (DNA) external from the body. The data indicate that when individuals are in a heart-focused, loving state and in a more coherent mode of physiological functioning, they* *have a greater ability to alter the conformation (shape or structure) of DNA."- (2013).*

So, what the writer is demonstrating here is, our emotional traumas or emotional acceptances of love can be altered and have an effect on our bodies. DNA is our biological and physiological anatomy. Ever wonder why when you quote- unquote "fall in love" you feel squeezy? The heart rate rises and falls when you see, hear, or touch that person? Those are your physical responses within your nervous system experiencing anatomical changes. So, you can't see the mind, and will of your soul. But you can experience affections of love, hurt to your emotions. We know and understand from the writings of King David's Psalms to his son's writings in the Songs of Solomon, that love, and pain can go hand in hand. However, love never hurts anyone. It's our decisions to be unkind and cruel that brings it on. Loving someone is risky business. Love in of its self is not risky. However, love ignites our emotions, but love is not part of our emotions. Love is not an emotion, it's only an ignitor.

WHAT IS AN IGNITOR?

And ignitor is a substance used to ignite or kindle a fire. It is a substance that burns that can easily start a coal or stoke a fire, kindling or tinder (we are in essence the coal, kindle or tinder). An ignitor powers a lamp, or transformer. We are spiritual lamps the lights, the Holy Spirit are our ignitor. Imagine a match stick and a matchbox in your mind. The match stick is us and love is the matchbox. Unless the match stick strikes the matchbox, you will never get the desired result (FIRE). The matchbox receives the friction of the match sticks infusion. Unless we act, love will just wait. When we are doers performing our acts of services or physical touches, love ignites a response. One cannot be without the other. God designed us to be a kind of match stick, or candles when struck or lit on the matchbox (love), we fire up. This fused action is what causes us to be human and spiritual beings.

You risk losing a part of yourself each time you are struck by a touch of love. But you also gain the benefits and rewards of experiencing the power of loving. Whether you want to call it an investment, a risk, a trial period etc., it involves you extending a vital part of self to become ignited. You're in one of the most vulnerable positions the heart is subjected too. How to love beyond pain is not only an after effect, but on many occasions and more so it's during the intimate relationship effects. Affection and touching through hugs and kisses, having that human contact is like a drink of a fresh glass of water. Unless you continue to fuel love by acts of giving its power is subject to burn out. The relationship starts out harmoniously sweet. You are very much into each other, or if it's your child you nurture and love him or her through development. It could be a mentor that you look up to deeply or some other relative that you are close to. No matter what brings you in the relationship, there you are at risk of being hurt. It's a part of life, how does anyone escape it? For God so loved the world that He gave (John 3:16), think about it, a supreme being loved His creation so much that He wanted to make the connection between creation and creator. God never experienced sin, never felt the effects of sins of others, never looked on sin. Through Jesus, the creator became the creation.

So, how does an awesome God make such a reckless decision and why? Remember, love speaks, and love does. God, spoke the word and everything we see and know was formed into existence. When he spoke it, he saw it, it was created. His love was 3-fold, speak, see, and do. When we place so much time an effort into anything, we become a part of it. We too, speak, see, and do. Love cannot act any other way. Love performs, produces, gives, creates. When love is ripped away something seems to tear at the soul. The pain is so greatly felt for some, a physiological occurrence takes place to the body. The body feels the pain through the soul's experiences. Your spirit stands by waiting to see what will happen next. The spirit can be quenched by the actions of the body and soul. In 1 Thessalonians 5:19, 23 states, "quench not the Spirit" "And the very God of peace sanctify you wholly; and I pray God your whole spirit and soul and body be preserved blameless until the coming of our Lord Jesus Christ"

It's not that the Spirit of God feels emotional pains. But this quenching spoken of is a sort of drawing back from that which is sinful or lacks the characteristics of. The Spirit of God doesn't engage in any sinful acts the body and soul wants to do. Therefore, this quenching is not an emotional feeling rather it's an act of His love withdrawing from the works of the soul, mind and body. When the scriptures speak of our spirit, we are made up of body, soul and spirit. Our spirit responds in the same manner as His Spirit. These two 'spirits,' or 'Spirits,' have no emotional human response mechanisms only an action that readies to stand up or stands back or away from that which it can or cannot relate. When we die, our body goes back to dust, our soul or conciseness is still aware and goes to the place assigned by God, and our spirit goes back to God. In Romans 8:16, "the Spirit himself testifies or bare witness with our spirit that we are God's children." 1 Corinthians 2:11 says, "For what man knows the things of a man except by the spirit of the man which is in him? Even so no one knows the things of God except by the Spirit of God." A human being is given a spirit by God and is not conscious of itself but works in connection with our human brains. Our brains make us humans from all other beast and creatures. It gives us the ability to understand, reason, speak language, writings, math, and sounds. We are fearful and wondrously made. The image of God is his essence, his presence, and ability to create life or destroy it. Our human bodies are not His image that so many think we are. When Jesus said, if you have seen me you have seen the Father also, he wasn't speaking about his human form. That's one of the reasons they wanted to stone him.

In Psalms 51: 5-11 A psalm of David, regarding the time Nathan the prophet came to him after David had committed adultery with Bath-Sheba.

5For I was born a sinner

yes, from the moment my mother conceived me.

6But you desire honesty from the womb,

teaching me wisdom even there.

7Purify me from my sins and I will be clean;

wash me, and I will be whiter than snow.

8Oh, give me back my joy again; you have broken me now

let me rejoice.

9Don't keep looking at my sins. Remove the stain of my guilt.

10Create in me a clean heart, O God. Renew a loyal spirit within me.

11Do not banish me from your presence, and don't take your Holy Spirit from me.

The key to loving beyond pain is to get renewed in spirit. The process of renewal is up to you. Going to God, asking for forgiveness of sins towards another takes humbling courage. When your soul is elevated, your spirit will be also. This means you're having to let go of anger, bitterness, resentment, discouragement, discontentment, frustration, vengefulness, all bad emotions. Making that connection realigns your spirit back with His Spirit. All future and subsequent actions now belong to Him. When some say, "I NEED A PHYSICAL TOUCH FROM GOD" what is being requested is a presence of His Spirit to invade our body, mind, and soul to restore our spirit fully. We are asking for a transcending above this natural world into something so powerful, that it interrupts our very life. Something so noticeable, that the sense is quickened within. A life changing spiritual experience.

How to love beyond pain? means suffering through it, bearing the scares while trying to move through the emotional storm. Having a heart of love despite it all. Reaching out to love and be loved through the powerful example of Jesus life. I experienced loneliness like never during my 5-year separation from my ex-husband. Even during our marriage, I needed so much attention from him. It seemed like everything and everyone else was so much more important than I. We were in ministry together, we had established a church and we formed a foundation and did community work together. However, something was missing. There was no physical touching, no quality time, giving was oftentimes for others and not us. Through my times of loneliness. I made poor decisions that cost me everything. I longed to be held and loved. Pain is not only felt during a break-up. It's felt when your together and needs are not met. I'm sure it's safe for me to say that I didn't fulfill all his needs either. We both were ministry focused, purpose-driven and not God-centered and oneness within our marriage.

Two people can live together and feel so much emotional pain and never know the other is in pain. Two people can sleep in the same bed never experiencing each other's heavy hearts. A marriage is not designed for silence. It's not meant for loneliness and separation. Yet, we say we are filled with the Holy Spirit that leads and guides us. NO, the fault is ours, not the Holy Spirit when we act contrary to His will. If you marry, don't ever forget you stood and took an oath before God and the congregation or witnesses that you would love each other. Loving means placing the well-being and interest of him or her before your own. It doesn't mean that a person should give up their goals and dreams; however, everything each one does should include the other in some form or another. It should be celebrated and appreciated. You create your own happiness, but you share it with the one you said you love.

Pain is defined as:

Psychological pain or mental pain is an unpleasant feeling (a suffering) of a psychological, non-physical, origin. A pioneer in the field of suicidology,

Edwin S. Shneidman, described it as "how much you hurt as a human being It is mental suffering; mental torment."

Psychological pain - Wikipedia
https://en.wikipedia.org/wiki/Psychological_pain

Emotional pain disrupts the soul's emotional wellness and the body's physical responses. Pain that is felt deeply can cause serious sicknesses. It can trigger diseases within. How does a person survive it? Imagine being in a vast ocean, and someone takes you on what you thought was a pleasant joy ride for the day. This person that you loved encouraged you, and swayed you, and enticed you to join him or her on this boat ride. Once there, him or her pushed you out of the boat into the ocean. Leaving you alone, and helpless you are stunned and in shock. You see the shore from a distance, but you have no boat to get back. You feel fear, panic, disbelief. Your mind tells you to go into survival mode. In a matter of minutes, if not seconds you begin to swim for your life. You're not thinking about pains of any kind. You go into fight or flight mode. You're thinking, I'm I hurt? How will I get to the safety of the shore? Who will rescue me, where will help come from? All these vitally important questions come to mind. You begin to move if you can swim great, but if not, you will die for sure. Surviving emotional pains are similar. You walk and run while wounded because you want to survive. However, if you don't want survival death is imminent.

So, what do you do? 'SINK OR SWIM?' emotional pain can bring you to your knees at a moment's notice. Your behaviors will change instantly, you breathe heavily, and your mind speeds up as if you were running a marathon. You make snap decisions, you cry out. The full effects have not surfaced yet. All you can think about is, how will I survive? Just like being out in the ocean, you move. To deal with emotional pain, you must be present. You must be mindful, in the now. Allow yourself to become present with your pains, but proactive with responses. Let whatever emotional pain you are feeling be felt but deal with it. I would caution here and say, if your pains are so great that you feel to harm yourself in any way, please seek help from your pastor, a counselor, or trusted friend. Don't allow pain to be so deeply felt within you that you lose hope. (Proverbs 13:12, 13 says) "Hope deferred makes the heart sick, but a dream fulfilled is a tree of life. People who despise advice are asking for trouble; those who respect a command will succeed." (NLT).

Love is like a fingerprint in some ways. A person has imprinted a part of him or her into your mind. Sharing that intimacy creates what is known as "soul ties". An impression is made that you will never be able to erase. You will never be able to remove it. You forgive, you develop a higher level of love that is forgivable in nature understanding the weakness and ignorance of that person. You get the mind of Christ within your mind, and you begin to see yourself loving as he would love. Remember, you are a spiritual being having an earthly experience. You're a spiritual tree planted by the many rivers of spiritual waters. The rivers of life are Christ blood your roots are wide and deeply rooted in Him. The imprint of that person, or persons will begin to be hoisted up from the roots of your soul. They will come through the trunk of your spiritual bosom as you pray for them. And, like leaves sprouting out from the branches of trees, your fruit from your spiritual limbs will see them as God sees. The bible tells us to pray for our enemies and those that persecute us and spitefully uses us.

You will gain insight into the Spirit of Christ love. His love is one of compassion, fully understanding the weaknesses and ignorance of mankind. Once you've grasped and accepted this human condition you will sense a new release within your soul. You will be enlightened within your spirit that humans do things intentionally and unintentionally to harm others. When they hurt you intentionally, this is a behavior having full cognition and awareness of wrongdoings. This is their human weaknesses at work because they lack truth about who God is and who you are. When they hurt you unintentionally, without cognition or awareness, then this is their ignorance. Most times, we have to forgive people for their ignorance. Jesus words, "FATHER FORGIVE THEM FOR THEY NO NOT WHAT THEY ARE DOING," was meant for those that ordered and carried out his crucifixion. When Judas betrayed him, Peter denied him, and the other disciple hid in fear of the Romans and the High Priest, these behaviors were the weaknesses of self-preservation.

No one else should ever be the object of your pain. These types of feelings are displaced, and misplaced emotions. Don't give way to thoughts, emotions or imaginations that were never a part of the equation. This can only drive you mad. Creating people, places and things that were never there will only serve to torment your soul further. In this type of situation, the Bible tells us once again, "whatsoever things are true, whatsoever things are honest, whatsoever things are just, whatsoever things are pure, whatsoever things are of good report; if there be any virtue, and if there be any praise, think on these things. Those things, which you have both learned, and received, and heard, and seen in me, do; and the God of peace shall be with you." (Philippians 4: 8, 9) Your emotions are a vital part of who you are as a person, therefore guard your soul, protect your body from what the mind of your thoughts wants to speak negatively. Sometimes, you must physically touch your own body. By this I mean, just like when a physical injury occurs to the body, your first reaction is to reach and grab the part that's wounded. Self-comfort is very appropriate in many cases of emotional pains. I tend to grab the back of my neck and massage it. No injury occurred there, but a way for me to alleviate emotional pain. I give myself a neck massage. And, if I'm really feeling deep pain, and I can afford it, I will go get a full body massage. Certain chemicals within the body are released when the body is touched.

All emotional pains are not equal. Emotional pains have varying degrees of pain. For instance, when I lost my mother, the pain as her daughter differed than when I lost my 2 brothers and my father. All were kin. But inside my emotions, the feelings of loss were not equal. I had a different type of relationship with my mother than I had with my father and brothers. Some will say, love is love, no, it's not. When I lost my spouse to divorce, that was another type of emotional pain. You see, we live in a world among others that we are closely knitted with. And so, when losses occur pain is felt immediately just in varying degrees and levels depending on the relationship. Can we stop loss, maybe sometimes? But it's a natural occurrence of life. This part of life as humans is hard to adapt and accept. Loving beyond pain, so you can live again requires courage. It requires faith and trust in God. It requires you, allowing yourself to be free from the chains of emotional ties that didn't work out. It requires forgiving and being forgiven. A decision must be made to live and to survive it. God in all His glory allowed Himself to be touched in every way to understand our humanist through Christ. Isaiah 53:3-5 King James Version (KJV) [3] He is despised and rejected of men; a man of sorrows and acquainted with grief: and we hid as it were our faces from him; he was despised, and we esteemed him not. Surely, he hath **borne our griefs**, and **carried our sorrows**: yet we did esteem him **stricken, smitten** of God, and **afflicted**. But he was **wounded** for our transgressions, he was **bruised** for our iniquities: the **chastisement** of our peace was upon him; and with **his stripes** we are healed. In every situation of emotional pain that I can remember I was feeling so wounded; it felt as though I would not survive it. When emotional pains hits, it first goes through the mind, will, and intellect which is your soul. You then literally feel your brains activities shifting and changing with every negative flow. Thoughts cloud your mind and seize or arrest your soul. To seize means, to take hold of suddenly and forcibly. It grabs hold of you and grips your soul. You have given it legal authority to take custody and possession of you. This is a type of spiritual military siege. It surrounds your body and becomes an enemy force that cuts off essential supplies of life for you to live. Crying uncontrollably and feelings of sadness and anxiety become debilitating. If you suffer from depression and anxiety these types of emotional hurts triggers and adds to what you're already experiencing. It's harder to recover and bounce back from. Persons on medications for depression or anxiety should continue to take them as directed by your physician. Never stop your medications because you are emotional distraught. This will only be a double whammy. Seek help from anyone that can see you through. If you're not on medications of this sort, try to relax and possibly see if you can get several full body massages over a period. The body needs positive stimuli in order to release 'endorphins.' "Endorphins are the body's natural opiates inducing feelings of wellbeing and reducing pain perception. They aid physical functions like breathing and heartbeat. Endorphins are among the brain chemical known as neurotransmitters, which function to transmit electrical signals within the nervous system. Endorphins interact with the opiates receptors in the brain to reduce our perception of pain and act similarly to drugs such as morphine and codeine" (Pain and Stress: Endorphins: Natural Pain and Stress Fighters, by medical authors Melissa Conrad Stoppler, MD: Medical Editor: William C. Shiel, Jr. MD, FACP, FACR. (1996). https://www.medicinenet.com

I experienced one of the toughest emotional upsets in my life. I was at a point if someone came in my home to rape or rob me or even kill me, I would have invited them with open arms. A very dangerous state of being. I didn't seek professional help because I wanted to die. I wanted the emotional pains to end. I wanted my body to be at rest. I was tired, so very tired of hurting. This was the seize, arrest, and siege I spoke of earlier. Nobody was there in my pain. I became a liability it seemed even to family. They didn't want to hear it or be around me. When family don't understand, don't fault them. God will send a friend. And He did!

Months and months went by where my heart would literally feel like it constantly quivered. Ached uncontrollably. It wouldn't stop, it wouldn't just go away. I cried to die, and I begged for deliverance. It only got worse. The pain grew to a point where I could not breathe. Anxiety and depression overtook me. All I could hear was the Lord saying to me, "I FORGAVE YOU, YOU FORGIVE IT." I still have an emotional reaction to cry when I think about these times. I think on forgiveness knowing I have forgiven it all. I'm pleasantly surprised to feel a physical touch from God's loving hand around me. Jesus made His acquaintance with all my grief and all my sorrows. For my transgressions, my sins He died and paid a price.

REFLECTION & NOTES

Chapter Three

Meeting a person for the very first time is like a clean canvas with fresh paint and paint brushes as I like to describe the encounter. You get to paint a picture together. You know nothing about him or her other than what's seen outwardly. So, with some kind gesture or *acts of service,* you seek to discover who this person really is. In the love language of *'Acts of Service,'* in most relationships you seek to please the person you want to give love actions towards. One of the questions you might ask, "Is there anything I can do for you, or anything I can get you?" It's so funny, how these kind of gestures get lost after a while.

However, let's look at it from an emotional painful perspective. For example, how likely are you to ask a person that has injured your soul, can I help you? Is there anything I can get you? Do you need anything? It's almost laughable isn't it? If anything, you'll want to tell that person to get the HELL out of your life, right? If love is an action word, isn't it supposed to go beyond words, wherein acts of services can still apply? Then whose love should we be operating in? The reason why I can bring this up it's not only from my own personal experiences, but I also watch my mother until the day my father died commit to acts of services. No matter how brutal, how ugly, how mean, how abusive my dad was towards my mom, she continued to demonstrate love. There were times in my life I hated my mom for being so loyal and so loving. The pain she endured and the psychological suffering we encountered to the degree had effects on me. I watched my mother cook, clean, sit lonely and alone. She was unloved and ignored by her husband my father, and yet she showed forth the love of Christ.

The day came when my father was on his death bed, still mean as ever, still raising hell, and my mother all day and night showed him love and served him. Her acts of services were the type of love that went beyond words, it went beyond emotional pains. When you're hurt to the core, into the depths of your soul, can you love beyond your own pains to serve someone that's the center of that pain? Every day of my mom's life, she rose up early in the mornings and prepared her day. Mother did not miss a beat in acts of courage and love for her husband, her children, and her neighbors. I never understood this behavior or level of love from her as a youth. Today in some regards, I'm pretty much like her. This is not to say mom didn't get angry or protest, she did. The point is, she never stopped in her love, kindness or acts of services for her husband, family and others despite her pains. I hated how my dad after 64 years of marriage treated my mom. However, my love for God was tested too one day. I came home from work one day, and I was tired. I was living with my parents back then. I went into the living room to sit down, and just before I could sit all the way down the Holy Spirit spoke. He said, "Go into your father's room and lead him to me." Writing this even now is hard for me, it's emotionally and overwhelming. I went into the room where my father was laying. I sat down beside him. I scooped my father into my arms and said these words. I said, "We will be okay, mom will be ok. If you want to go home to be with the Lord, it's okay now." I told my father, "Please try to repeat these words after me, and everything will be ok." My dad could barely speak at this time during his illness, because he had bone cancer throughout his body.

God allowed his lips and tongue to be released and move as he spoke after me. "Father, in Jesus name, please forgive me." If you could only had seen how desperately my dad wanted to utter those words. When I tried to take my dad through the completeness of Romans 10:9, he had no strength to do so. What was important, my father reckoned with his Lord the day before he died and asked for forgiveness of sins. He said, "PLEASE FORGIVE ME." Acts of services of love might save someone's life. Even though, people in your life might have hurt you all your life and have hurt others, love beyond your pains for restoration. You need to be restored, and they need your forgiveness whether they realize it or not. Jesus' last act of service on this earth was giving His life to pay for our sins. He did us a great service of love when He forgave it all. I left that day for Virginia. When I arrived there, I got a call my father was dead. I lifted my hands towards heaven and began to weep and praise God. I said, "Thank you Lord for saving my dad. I praise you for forgiving him before he left this world." I was overjoyed that while I had pains from my father's actions towards my mother and us; I was able to yield my broken soul and with love and obedience listened to the voice of God. God loved him more than I ever could. We must believe that while people close to us hurt us God still loves them too. His salvation doesn't stop because we are in pain. He died for the just and unjust. The fruit of our trees are not always for us to receive nourishment. It's for those that come in contact with our lives or even just passing by. The fruit of love, patience, peace, joy, happiness, longsuffering, mercy and self-control provides harmony for us all.

Are you able to forgive beyond any selfish acts that were committed against you? Are you able to love beyond whatever emotional pains you are feeling right now? Will you allow the Lord to heal you while He's operating on your soul and move on? It takes dying to self, it takes hurting, healing and loving all at the same time. It takes the Holy Spirit to show you the bigger picture of pain to the soul and loving beyond it all. The old song goes, "He looked beyond all my faults and saw my needs" this is so sweet to me. My faults were many and my sins were great. The word of God tells us, in Psalms 103: 1, "As far as the east is from the west, so far hath he removed our transgressions from us." (KJV) Love is an action word isn't it? It requires moving, putting forth an effort. When we say that we have Christ love, we must also have Christ actions. I'm not trying to downplay the difficulties of loving someone that has hurt you. However, to spare your soul, what I am trying to say is, be alert, be aware of where your soul is at. Pain can consume you with bitterness and hatred. Emotional hurt can take over your life if you're not careful to release it. Give it away to God, He's the only one that can fix it. Be willing and allow Him. There are numerous occasions I could write about when my mother loved beyond her pains. I believe, my mother loved God so much that she loved herself. In loving herself she loved others. The fruit of the Spirit is love, joy, peace, longsuffering, gentleness, meekness, goodness. These attributes belong to the Spirit of God. As a believer, they must also be in you.

Your *'Acts of Service'* requires them. How else will you be able to serve? Give self-love before serving others love. The experience must be uniquely experienced between you and God first before you can genuinely provide it to others. I'm inspired within myself whenever I feel the presence of God's love. It's something indescribable. I also think we all know His presence differently because He knows how to give each of us what we need. I feel Him right now as I'm writing this passage. I'm overcome with His love, His warmth telling me, "I'm here, I love you as no one else can." 'If I told you everything I ever did, would you still love me?' was a message I spoke on some years ago. What I know is, not everyone and very few will continue to love and serve you if they knew all you ever did. Even though you have been forgiven, and restored, some people find it difficult reaching to that level of love. However, our Father has no qualms about it, He just does it. We see *'Acts of Services'* sometimes as condoning one's behaviors. No, see them as God sees them and it eliminates any thoughts of that. I keep going back to my mother because she was my primary human example. It wasn't just my father where she displayed kindness after wrongs done, it was family, people in ministry especially, friends in her community that betrayed her love. It was her children that hurt her. As one of her daughters, I'm sure I hurt her too because of my own pains.

Writing this book is hard for me. I stop frequently to cry.   While the pain of loving beyond pains is challenging and difficult to bare, God gives us the grace and courage to face self and others despite it all. I think about the hurt I caused others, something I'm not proud of. It's something that stays with me as a reminder to never take those that love me for granted. I think of my ex-husband Greg he loved me, we had many issues and I found it hard loving him and serving him. If I could erase it all and show one Act of Service of love and kindness to him again, I would be grateful and honored. Countless, '*Acts of Service*' can fill an ocean where men and women loved beyond pain from the time of humanity's existence. True love begins from the heart of God. We are created in His image. Therefore, it's built within us to love no matter what. It's our willingness to yield that interrupts this flow. Pain can turn us into another person all together causing us to do and say ugly things under any normal circumstances we would not do or speak.

Therefore, the Holy Spirit as our guide is necessary to our spiritual growth and development. And I would dare say, even after being filled we still must yield because the ways of the flesh must be crucified daily. At any moment, any time we can choose to step outside the Holy Spirit's guidance and as the Bible states, "Return back to your own vomit." Take yourself through a little test next time an opportunity arises wherein you have been hurt by someone you're close to. Show an act of service beyond what your emotions are presently feeling. If you begin to practice this, you will find it's possible to allow love to lead you through the acts of giving services. Don't think about the pain, the lies, the disappointments. I encourage and press you to think about Jeremiah 31:3, "The Lord appeared to us in the past, saying, I have loved you with an everlasting love; therefore, with lovingkindness have I drawn thee." The love of Jesus is bigger than any emotion you are being challenged or bombarded with in your mind right now. Tell your soul to be at peace. Still the soul, and with a love that's greater than pain, forgive it. If you are going through, ask God to help you through.

THE BIG
THUMBS-UP

As a reminder, I give myself a Big Thumbs-Up.

This signifies I point upward to seek His strength to love

beyond pain, so I can live again!

My friends, say this prayer with me:

-Father, I come to you in your name Jesus. I affirm and acknowledge that for me to love beyond pain, I must love with your love. I must forgive with the Spirit you embodied when you died. I ask that you raise my spirit above all hurt, pain, lies, deceit, and disappointments committed against me. That you forgive me for any wrongs I may have committed towards others. If there is anything in me that is not pleasing before you, I ask that you show it to me, and help me to deal with it. Lord, I ask that you teach me about the love you had when you died. The love that kept you on the cross, the love that took you 3 days in the pits of hell, the love that raised you up where you ascended on high. Give me that love that goes beyond any pain I could ever experience in this life, so I can live again both naturally and spiritually in you. Amen-

Sometimes, we don't get it, we don't comprehend this kind of love at all. Speaking from my own experiences only a very small fraction of this type of love I've come to understand. When a person can lie, deceive, betray, disappoint, cause loss, and near life and still reach-out to his or her detractor this is truly loving. This is walking in the fruit of God's Spirit of love. It does not mean that all human responses won't try to arise and take control of the mind and flesh. But the Spirit will have precedence, authority to reign in the situation first. I'm overcome with fullness in my heart. I want my grandchildren, and my great-grandchildren to hear of this great love story from their grandmother. I want them to learn how to love beyond pain too. It's my hope that one day they will find this book and read it. I desire to leave a legacy of love for them.

So much is happening in my life and has happened. There were events and actions that occurred that I couldn't ever tell anyone. The silence of my soul agonized with grief. When family or friends hurt you, it's hard to trust them with any further pains in your life. When they are the offenders, it's hard to share those things that family should know you are experiencing. As you read further, and as you take this journey with me in this book everything will be revealed. Acts of Services will not always be understood by others or accepted. You can never explain to others why you did this or did that. Or why didn't you do that or the other? We give our souls over to people that do not have our entire best interest at heart. We foolishly 'love' those that need to be delivered from selfish and self-seeking agendas. So, let me be clear, I don't believe in same sex marriages. I'm a believer, and I believe what the word of God states about a man and a woman's union. What I want to say is, within this book, you will read a story, a story about two people's lives. You may or may not agree with the events that took place in their lives, but the point in sharing it over the pages to come, is to show you how love; being the root in the foundation of light and love, supersedes all other acts. It's the hinge where everything else swings. This will be discussed in the up and coming chapters.

REFLECTION & NOTES

Chapter Four

Now, let's continue to discuss the next language, *'Gifts & Giving.'* In the book of Mark 9:38-41, Jesus speaking to His disciples about using the name of Jesus had this conversation. "John said to Jesus, "Teacher, we saw someone using your name to cast out demons, but we told him to stop because he wasn't in our group." Don't stop him Jesus said. "No one who performs a miracle in my name will soon be able to speak evil of me. Anyone who is not against us is for us. 41. If anyone gives you even a cup of water because you belong to the Messiah, I tell you the truth, that person will surely be rewarded." (NLT)

I brought this scripture up to demonstrate to you that even when you are not acknowledged openly by another's Jesus sees a labor of love. The rewards of giving a cup of water is rewarded because of whose you are. In the following scriptures, it further speaks on harming the little one's (His children) that trust in Him. He said, "It is better that you be thrown in the sea and a large millstone placed around your neck." So, you might say, "How do I give to a person that has offended me or another?" Jesus also said, "Father forgive them for they know not what they are doing." He tells us to love our enemies and pray for those that use us and persecute us. Sounds like a contradiction doesn't it? Love is multi-directional. It turns on all axels of a wider enlightenment of ones understanding to know the truth. The next time someone harms you, think about their weaknesses and ignorance as being their problem not yours.

In the following scriptures, Jesus talks about how everyone will be tested by fire. Fire is a consuming element, it burns out and destroys whatever is in its path. Spiritual fires are a few things. The Holy Spirit will baptize you, not with water, but with fire (SPIRIT) so you can have the power to do what He has assigned for you. He's called the Holy Spirit which is God's anointing in you and upon you. The other is found in 1 Peter 1:7. "These trials will show that your faith is genuine. It is being tested as fire. Tested and purified as gold though your faith is far more precious than mere gold. So, when your faith remains strong through many trials, it will bring you much praise and glory and honor on the day when Jesus Christ is revealed to the whole world." (NLT) When you continue to give, the very act of giving is a gift. Test comes in all types and forms in our lives. Fire is used here as something transforming. It is a gift from God to shape and mold you for His use. You might be asking God to give you more patience. Patience is a gift from God, it doesn't just show up and say here I am my name is patience. Patience comes before during and after a trial. After the trial, you are given this gift to present, not to keep. Can you continue loving self and forgiving another so that patience can be developed in you? Our Father will deal severely with those that harm us, but He wants us to live in peace. Living in peace means, forgiving, and being forgiven. If a situation arises that emotionally damages you, will you allow the Lord to work the patience within you required, so you can love again?

Love is the greatest gift of all the spiritual gifts spoken about in 1 Corinthians. Love beyond pain, so you can live again is the gift that keeps on giving and giving. When you can love someone that hurt you, lied, and deceived you after winning your heart; that gift opens the heart of the soul of the offender to receive God's love.

From the Father's heart, through your heart, to the offender's heart, it travels like a vein so very far. When Jesus cursed the fig tree, He cursed it because it was not bearing fruit in its season and within its' design. It was time to feed the passerby. It was time for all those travelers to be able to pluck its fruits to be fed, to receive nourishment. We all fall into seasons and phases in life that are not favorable. We stop in our tracks, we don't feel like growing anymore. We get discouraged, and life sucks for sure. But, just like that fig tree, if we stop doing what God has purposed and designed in our lives, the work ends, and we will dry up and die. I'm in so much emotional pain writing this book at times. However, I must, somebody need to know they can walk and run while wounded. They can make it through whatever their emotional hurts are. I've been lied to, deceived, stolen from, swindled, but I rise. I rise to love and be loved and show forth the glory of God. Do I want to dry up and die....? YES, I DO. But what would be the benefit in that? Who would continue to suffer? Where would my life end up? I choose to love beyond my pains, love the offender, and forgive with the love of Jesus.

The person that hurt me with many arrows called me crying and weeping asking for forgiveness just the other day. God's mercy was being challenged in me for what was done to me. I was asked to pray and forgave it all. I wept and cried uncontrollably for days too. I prayed a prayer of forgiveness and healing and restoration. The gift of forgiveness is what I gave, the fruit from my tree. The pain remained, but forgiveness was working its way through every layer of hurt and wrongs done. Two weeks passed by, and full healing was completed for us both.

This was the hardest time for me, truly it was. I decided, I'm going to love beyond my pains and reach out until God's work in me was done. You see, it's getting through, pushing through, and maintaining until it's through. Further in this book, I will share more about the healing power of God in this story that's so incredibly powerful when love stood through the storms beyond my emotional pains.

REFLECTION & NOTES

CHAPTER 5

Have you ever watched one of those movies where a man is wounded by a knife, bullet, and some other object? Notice how once a wound is inflicted, he gets back up and keep on fighting or walks until he's in a safe place or gets help right? Dealing with emotional pain is like that and for your healing, you must spend *quality time* in prayer and fasting to get your next set of instructions. Depending on what type of wound it might be at the end of the story he survives it. If the wound is not fatal generally there is time to recover. However, you still must stay in the moment to treat the wound, you can't just check out. Spend *quality time* with Jesus get revived. The 23rd Psalms is about spending *quality time* in the green pastures with the Father.

The LORD is my shepherd; I shall not want.

2 He maketh me to lie down in green pastures: he leadeth me beside the still waters.

3 He restoreth my soul: he leadeth me in the paths of righteousness for his name's sake.

⁴ Yea, though I walk through the valley of the shadow of death, I will fear no evil: for thou art with me; thy rod and thy staff they comfort me.

⁵ Thou preparest a table before me in the presence of mine enemies: thou anoint my head with oil; my cup runneth over.

⁶ Surely goodness and mercy shall follow me all the days of my life: and I will dwell in the house of the LORD forever.

The Lord as your shepherd is one that guides and protects, keeps from harm of those that will prey upon you. The Lord makes you, he urges and nudges you to lay down in green pastures with him as he leads you to the waters that will heal your wounded soul. He restores your soul back to the SPIRIT FILLED RESILENCY is was originally in before it was injured. The only paths he can take you down is those of right living and Christ-like attributes because Jesus is His name sake. And, even though you will walk through the weakness and ignorance of others who have hurt your soul to the point of death, He tells you to fear no other evil that will come against you, for they will surely come. But He is with you, and His rod of correction and staff that He will raise a standard against your enemy, will comfort you and you will see His hand at work. Every day, He prepares a table of His love before you if you get in His presence to feast upon His goodness and mercy. He will openly do this in the presence of all those that hurt you and offended your soul. God is so good, He will even anoint your head with oil in their presence, and they will see your cup of His goodness running over. God's sheep-dogs, GOODNESS & MERCY are with you everywhere you go all the days of your life until He's ready to call you home. After that, you will dwell in the house of the Lord forever. Your home, be at peace and rest your soul in His house. Amen!

But, let's get back to how to walk and run while wounded. I'm going to describe to you 5 types of wounds all survivable, but some more severe than others. Then, I'm going to draw a parallel in contrast to these wounds to emotional wounds to the soul.

> "A wound is a type of injury which happens relatively quickly in which skin is torn, cut, or punctured (an open wound), or where blunt force trauma causes a contusion (a closed wound). In pathology, it specifically refers to a sharp injury which damages the dermis of the skin." (Stephanie Chandler, 2014).

https://en.wikipedia.org/wiki/Wound

According to Stephanie Chandler (2014), there are 5 types of wounds. Now that we have defined what a wound is, we will use contrast and correlations which are part of the core subject of this book as to how the soul, mind, and body is affected. As any adult knows all too well, wounds occur in countless ways and very broadly in severity. A wound generically refers to a tissue injury caused by physical means. In everyday parlance, wounds typically refer to skin injuries. Medical professionals classify skin wounds in several ways, such as whether they are short- or long-term, and whether they are contaminated with bacteria. These distinctions reflect differences in the nature, cause and likely course of the wound, as well as treatment decisions. Short-term, open wounds are often described in 5 categories, based on the mechanism and appearance of a skin injury. (Chandler 2014). https://www.livestrong.com/article/101274-five-types-wounds/

So, let's talk about this first wound, then make some spiritual correlations as it pertains to the soul. Wounded souls should continue to give from their hearts despite their wounds. This is a hard process, but a necessary one in order to be like Jesus in his role of the great forgiver. Medical doctors note many types of physical wounds, but we will discuss 5 types of bodily wounds and correlate them to soul wounds.

INCISIONAL WOUND:

Become Enlighten, See it from a Spiritual Perspective

~An Incision wound refers to a clean cut in the skin caused by a sharp object. Accidentally cutting yourself with a kitchen knife, scissors or a piece of broken glass are everyday examples of incision wounds. A surgical incision is another common example. Incision wounds typically heal more quickly than other types of wounds because of the smooth skin edges. Scarring is also typically less extensive with deep incision wounds, compared to other types of deep skin wounds. ~ (Stephanie Chandler, 2014)

Whether self-inflicted or caused by another person, you were cut with what is called an incisional wound to the soul so-to-speak. An incision as explained above is a clean cut in the skin with a sharp object. It can be caused by yourself, or by some other broken object. In this case for spiritual correlations, we will say a broken soul caused an incisional wound. Someone said or done something to you. It was either on purpose or accidently. Either way, you're cut open right? Some other broken soul cut you and caused an incision to your soul. Now there are two broken souls with an incision. If you want to rise to the occasion of spiritual growth and development, you have a choice to make. Emotional pains are wounds to the soul left untreated, unattended, and unforgiven. The author above stated that typically, these wounds can heal more quickly than other types of wounds. Why, because of the smooth skin edges? Furthermore, she states that "scarring is also typically less extensive with deep incision wounds." (Chandler, 2014).

Now, in correlation to the soul, no doubt pain is pain, right? When you feel it, it is felt, and it hurts. This smooth skinned soul wound can be easily recoverable and healed quickly. It's survivable. In order, to survive this incision to the soul you must first forgive it immediately. I will always, always put this out first about forgiveness. There is no love without forgiveness, and no forgiveness ability without love. And without either of these, there is no healing or recovery. Just as the skin on our bodies are designed by God to be the first defense against the attack of infection or injury of any kind, love and forgiveness must be our first spiritual defense for the soul. An untreated wound of any kind to the soul will get infected and cause more damage to your mind. In the natural, when an incision wound happens, we clean it and place a band-aid on it. The soul wound such as someone said hurtful words, held your hand too tightly in anger, took something from you of value that was irreplaceable, or told a white lie; are small but still hurtful right? If these things are not addressed immediately, it keeps you feeling ill. The best gift you can give to anyone you love, is the opportunity to hear your heart. You have the right as a human being to be heard and validated for your injury. You have a right to address the hurt you feel out of no fault of your own. However, you do not have the spiritual right to retaliate in an ungodly manner according to scripture. You do not have the spiritual right to cause discord amongst other sisters and brothers who have no knowledge of your incident with the offending party. You do not have the spiritual right to be an assassinator of anyone's character and seek revenge towards the one that offended you. Give that person a chance for explanation, allowing him or her to ask for forgiveness.

The Bible instructs us in Matthew 18:15 which says, "Moreover if thy brother shall trespass against thee, go and tell him his fault between thee and him alone: if he shall hear thee, thou hast gained thy brother." In verse 16 it says, "But if they will not listen, take one or two others, so that in the mouth of two or three witnesses every word may be established. The third step if he or she will not hear you, it's further stated, and if he shall neglect to hear them, tell it unto the church: but if he neglects to hear the church, let him be unto thee a heathen man and a publican." (KJV). If we follow biblical instructions towards not only our sisters and brothers in Christ, but those that are without Christ, we would have a potential brother or sister and reconcile with those that are in the faith. Keeping emotions hidden will only drive a deeper wounded wedge between you. Gift giving is what God gave of himself through Jesus. He loved us so much that He gave Himself as a ransom for sins. Offenses are sins imposed on another. How many times should we forgive our brothers and sisters and those without Christ? The bible states 70 x 7=490 times a day.

LACERATION WOUND:

Become Enlighten, See it from a Spiritual Perspective

"A laceration refers to an injury caused by tissue tearing. Your skin is both tough and flexible, so it takes a lot of force to cause a laceration. Because of the high force involved, other deeper tissues such as bones, muscles, tendons, ligaments, blood vessels, nerves and even internal organs are frequently also damaged. Skin lacerations most frequently occur over bony prominences, like the elbows, knees and hips. Blunt trauma, such as occurs in a car accident or being hit with a hard object, is the most common mechanism of laceration injuries. Because the skin edges are jagged and torn, a laceration injury heals more slowly and with more scarring than an incision wound." (Stephanie Chandler, 2014)

Now, here with a type of laceration to the soul, you might be asking, how does anyone have the capacity to walk or even run with these types of wounds? Let's visit a story about Jesus in John chapter 19. In St. John chapter 19 beginning at the first verse it states, "Pilate took Jesus and had him beaten. The soldiers made a big ring of thorns like a crown and put it on Jesus' head. They put a red gown on him. They said, Greetings, King of the Jews! Then, they beat him with their hands, and he was also whipped until his skin was torn to the bones; he was unrecognizable." (KJV) A description of a (Flogging), you're stripped naked, with 2 people on each side taking turns. You're whip with what is called "cat-o-nine tails that consisted of 18-inch-long leather straps about 6 or 7 feet long. At the end of each strap was small lead balls mixed with pieces of animal bones or metal. These would tear into the skin and each successive lashing the jagged bones from dead animals' tears through the flesh. Vital organs down to the spine were sometimes revealed. Stop for a moment and imagine 40 lashes.

The physical pains Jesus endured on that day was gruesome, to put it mildly brutal. Prior to this beating, Jesus' heart must have been broken to his soul. In Matthew, it talked about his betrayal and arrest. Being betrayed breaks something so far deep inside you that the feeling has a gross saddening effect. When you give your love freely, give your possessions freely, deprived yourself of basic needs willingly; and that person don't consider you at all, it's devastating. After he was taken to the High Priest house, its further noted how Jesus was struck in the face by an officer of the High Priest. In addition, he was blindfolded, then beaten and spat on by the men around him, the Bible tells us (Jn. 18:22 KJV). Sometimes, you can't see your enemies, but you can hear them, smell them, feel them touching you even in your mind. I must pause here and say that just writing this for the sake of making a point about walking and running while wounded strikes me to my soul.

How could Jesus bare this brutal attack both mentally, emotionally, and physically? What did it do to him in the flesh knowing this was to be his sacrifice of suffering to reconcile all generation? We can now see, how his word tells us to run with patience, to run and not be weary, to walk and not faint; that the trial of our faith is far more precious than of gold. Walking and running while wounded are profoundly demonstrated within these scriptures, as it lays before us love and forgiveness in rare and raw form. Imagine, having all power, and being all-powerful to crush and utterly-destroy those that are killing you? But, for love and forgiveness sake you keep, as he kept his mouth closed uttering not a word. I'm not condoning or saying that anyone should allow physical abuse or mental afflictions. However, the point here is it takes such love and forgiveness to overcome this level of wounds and pains. What I am also saying is, for your soul sake forgive it, and keep your heart of love open to be loved again so you can live. Jesus came so we might have life, and that more abundantly. Not just in the hereafter, but life and love now. We hurt because we cannot imagine those who love us to do the unthinkable towards us. But it happens, and we must live despite those pains. It's the soulish realm or part of us that is crippled when we are hurt, but we are much more than the soul. It's necessary to understand that the very part of us that gives us life is more than the part of us that gives us our ability to reason, think, and process information.

We think, at times and moments in our lives how impossible it is for us to forgive and love someone that caused us pain. We think, how much we want to die and bury our heads never to rise again due to hurt to the soul. Jesus clearly demonstrated his love towards us and walked the road of suffering and shame for sins he never committed. To pay a debt he never owed. He became a ransom which required blood. Lacerations to the soul are recoverable, but some are not. Surely, it will take the love of Christ to heal you if you don't give in to it all. You can rise and walk and run while wounded only with him at the center of your life. This theme will never change, love and forgive. Let them ground you and anchor your soul in the one that can make you whole again. JESUS! What are some deep soul lacerations we can extract from Jesus experiences here besides the beating he took you might be experiencing? Emotional abuse, betrayal, lies, deceit, thievery, false love and affections, name calling, deceptions, denials, hidden agendas, usurers, shaming, mocking. Physical abuse, strikes, battery to the body, spitting, slapping, kicking, use of hard objects, chocking, all abuse is abnormal behaviors and misuse of objects, for the purpose, of harming another. (If you are being subjected to any of these, tell someone, anyone).

ABRASIONAL WOUND:

Become Enlighten, See it from a Spiritual Perspective

An abrasion occurs when the skin is scraped off due to rubbing against a rough surface. A skinned knee or elbow is a common example of a minor, superficial abrasion wound. However, these skin wounds can be serious if the abrasions are deep or widespread, such as occurs after a fall from a motorcycle or a bicycle traveling at a relatively high speed. Commonly known as road rash or road burn, these injuries are often quite painful and sometimes require skin grafts to replace the lost skin. Scarring typically doesn't occur with superficial abrasions but can be extensive with deep abrasions. (Stephanie Chandler 2014)

Four words here, 'AGAINST A ROUGH SURFACE' most of us experience these types of wounds to our souls. It is through these 'rough surfaces' encounters that starts the ball rolling. There's a lot of revelation in abrasions to the soul I think can be extracted in a spiritual way. A superficial abrasion is common occurrences when sustaining a fall from a bike, or tripping on your shoe strings on a pavement. The writer mentions these falls as road rashes and road burns. Everyone had a carpet burn? This is an abrasion to the skin's surface. It's painful, it hurts and it stings. If the abrasion is bad enough the writer states, some need skin grafts when the abrasion is deep. Abrasions to the surface of your most intimate being like a skin abrasion is felt immediately. There is an instant shock to the mind and your first natural reaction is to grab the surrounding skin near the circumference of that wound. You utter words to try to console or express what you're experiencing.

You hold it, your eyes well up with tears, and your trembling. You get frustrated with what just happened. There's this disbelief that invades your mind like, "What in the world? How in the world did that happen?" People in your life will hurt you, no surprise there. They will say hurtful words such as, you're worthless, I hate you, and your nothing. Words like, I want a divorce, I'm leaving you. You don't make me happy, I'm not happy with you, I'm leaving you for another person. All kinds of soulish abrasions happen every single day all day long. Think about the millions of souls walking around hurt inside because of words said. Skin abrasions, soul abrasions attack the mind and you just can't figure out why or what just happened. You know who and when, but why? It happened suddenly.

Beloved, the great thing about God is, He's able to heal from the inside out, and the outside in. When you sustain a soul abrasion what should you do? Well, like skin abrasions, if it's on the surface you get some soap and water clean it up. You place an ointment such as Neosporin or similar products to keep infections out. You might or might not cover it with a band-aid. You sit down and take a few moments, so pain can ease from it. Then, after a while, you stand up and you walk. You mobilize yourself again because first, the pain has lessened, your thoughts are gathered, you've applied medication and gauzes to the area and you're ready to go again. Soulish surface abrasions are similar. The question is HOW do I begin? First, you clean your soul from the filth of words placed in your mind by another. You apply scriptures from the word of God like an ointment of truth. You examine yourself by assessing if what was said had any truth in it. You dissect it through the spirit of your mind. You ask yourself hard questions and see if there be any truth to it. If so, ask God to help you transform your behaviors into what's pleasing to Him. If not, then don't allow it to settle in your soul. It's a lie, give no place to the negativity or opinions of other hurt souls. It has nothing to do with the devil and everything to do with a weak and ignorant hurt soul of the offender.

What does God say about you? How does He feel about you? What did Jesus do in these types' situations? Where in scripture do, I go concerning healing and words of affirmation and faith? Then, you stand, and you walk it through with love and forgiveness in your heart. Don't cover it with hate, self-pity resentment, revenge, bitterness, malice, strife, contention, but the love band-aid cover you. Deeper abrasions might take a little more of each of these applications and possibly a soulish skin graft. Replace old soulish ties and hurts and pains with new relationships that are healthy, vibrant and productive. Ones that will celebrate you and not hurt you. Deep soulish abrasions can put you under at times and incapacitate you even. But, like any of the other wounds, they are recoverable if you let go, and let God heal you. The first order is to love and forgive it all, then run and not be weary. Because we are human, we absorb too much traffic in our soul's system. Use your spiritual brakes and stop signs by putting on the whole armor of God.

AVULSIONAL WOUND:
Become Enlighten, See it from a Spiritual Perspective

Skin avulsion, also known as degloving, is a serious injury in which the skin is torn from the tissues beneath it. The mechanism of skin avulsion typically involves the skin catching on an object while the involved body part is in motion. Ring avulsion, such as occurred to comedian Jimmy Fallon, is an example. Depending on the circumstances of injury, avulsed skin can sometimes be surgically reattached. If reattachment is not possible, skin grafts are typically used to replace the lost tissue. (Stephanie Chandler, 2014)

An Avulsion is a very, very serious wound as stated by the writer. It's the type of wound which the skin is torn from the tissue beneath. I want to carefully dissect this one because this type of wound occurs while everything is in motion. You might say, life is good, and all seems well. In the description of this wound, your body is moving in a direction pushing against gravity and the forces around it. Wow, so how can we describe this from a soulish spiritual perspective?

There are unseen forces constantly at work against the children of God. I really had to process this one to think about it from a spiritual correlation within scripture. In Ephesians 6:12 says, "We wrestle not against flesh and blood, but against principalities, against powers, against the rulers of the darkness of this world, against spiritual wickedness in high places." (KJV) The first few words here really explain the offenses that people do in their weaknesses and ignorance. As far as not fighting against "Flesh and Blood," weaknesses are the quality or feature regarded as a disadvantage or the state or condition of lacking strength. Ignorances are lack of knowledge or information. So as children of God, our fight is not against the soul hurters for their weaknesses and ignorance, but the fight is more against principalities.

What are principalities? A principality is a state ruled by a prince or sometimes princedom. A prince from a certain kingdom or authority which there is an order of angles. The word "Powers "are both good and bad in scope to spiritual activities. Spiritual powers in faith are in a higher supreme being we know as God even though that name God was assigned by the Greeks in Babylonian times 6[th]century BCCE. We look to God to be our consciousness and guide offering to us a sense of peace, contentment, confidence and hope that loving and positive. What are evil powers? These are powers that have a vast assortment of evil and malicious spirits assigned to make war against the work and people of God. These powers are seen and unseen, meaning they are in operation within false teachers, prophets with demonic entities that empower them. 'Rulers of Darkness' in this world are the entire kingdom of darkness that is the whole realm of satanic rule. Those that were cast out and cast down by God which have powers over this world's atmosphere and governing systems. "Spiritual Wickedness" are false teachers, prophets, pastors, evangelist, apostles that speak both truth and lies for their own agendas over mankind. They are wolves in sheep clothing disgusting themselves to be from God to game the sheep of God. "We are as sheep led to the slaughter" these people hid in the world's system of politics, and governments, and all authorities that can take power over any unsuspecting individual(s), or groups at will for their furtherment to rise on top and over people.

This story comes to mind, I won't use it to give its' full meaning only to draw a picture within your mind. The story is about Absalom the son of King David found in 2 Samuel 14:25 describing him as the following: Absalom or Avshalom, according to the Hebrew scriptures from the many sons of David, King of Israel along with Maacah, who was the daughter of Talmai, King of Gershur was depicted as the most handsome young man in all the kingdom. He had no blemishes from head to foot and only cut his hair once a year due to the weight of it. His name meant, "The Father of Peace" but Absalom was far from what his name truly meant. Absalom was known; however, for being a man who had the ability to win the heart of people thereby, winning loyalty and alliances. False teachers and prophets first order of the day is to win loyalty and gain alliances. Absalom, son of David rebelled against his father and attempted to have David killed and overthrown. One of King David's generals' Joab by name violated the Kings order not to harm Absalom and treat him gently. Joab chased Absalom on his horse. Now, here is where it gets interesting and deadly. An Avulsion wound remember is a wound caused by the body being in motion. The body is caught by an object that rips and tears the skin. This is a horrible of type wound. During Joab's hot pursuit of Absalom, Absalom's hair got caught up in the branches of a tree. It was said, his hair was so beautiful and curly that it added to his gorgeousness. All that beauty become his downfall. Sometimes, life can be so beautiful, so lovely, not a care in the world. In other instances, you could have it all and still be running from something or someone. While Absalom was in motion seated on his horse his hair got hung and he dangled from a tree. He got caught in the time of his life where he thought to gain power and life was going to be grand. Imagine that, imagine moving at such high-speed a part of you gets ripped off or seriously torn? As the story goes, Joab walked up to Absalom and pierced him through with his sword. Now, I only present this story to prepare your imagination for the wound called 'Avulsions' because it's just that bad. Remember, the mechanism of skin avulsion typically involves the skin catching on an object while the involved body part is in motion. Picture this, your married or in a relationship for several years. You have children, a mortgage, career, church ministry, community involvement, friends together, great neighbors and good health. You both are in leadership positions and everything is at stake. Or, your single and life is so good and the unthinkable happens? An avulsion wound to your soul can hit you out of nowhere.

Two souls intertwined and connect something happens within the DNA and biological chemicals begin changing. Earlier, we spoke about how this works scientifically as researchers studied these biological effects. Relationships are big responsibilities for all parties involved. Talking about flesh ripping away while in motion. Some relationships that are intimate a soulish avulsion wound takes place so violently it can be equated with skin being torn from inside the body while it's in motion. In Genesis 2:23 the scripture tells us, "The man said, this is now bone of my bone and flesh of my flesh she shall be called woman because she was taken from man." The tying of two souls is real. The gift of giving another person a part of your body and soul is also real; an incredible thing God designed us to do. To have the capability to give life is truly a gift from God. Being in a relationship is precious and should be respected.

The bond of two separate people is so fascinating and indescribable. The love and care that goes into relationships is a delicate and precious occurrence. But, as I was saying, something happens. It could be the death of a child, an affair, loss of a career, loss of the family home, spousal abuse or death of a spouse. Anything could just spring up at a time where life is lovely. We are all vulnerable to things happening beyond our control. So, how do you walk and run through an avulsion wound that is one of the top wounds discussed? The kind of wound where at one moment everything is fine, life is great, all is well? All I can say is, with patience by allowing the doors of patience to swing on the hinges of love and forgiveness and mercy. EASIER SAID THAN DONE.

You can't get that child back, your spouse has left you never to returned or has died suddenly or through illnesses, your career is over, everyone has turned their backs on you. You've lost everything and everyone you've ever known. One of my personal experiences is what I will share here. What I share can never be as bad as what others might go through, but it was bad for me. I had it all, a good husband; no not perfect, but he loved me. Nice furnished home, good job, family wasn't perfect, but they were there. Ministry and community were very much a part of living as one. Nice brand-new Camaro my dream car. Money wasn't in abundance, but I didn't want for nothing. I was in good health, and by all account's life seemed in order. However, like Absalom, there were areas of disobedience and rebellion. As a woman even though it seemed I had it all I was left alone a lot. I was sad, and no number of 'THINGS' could satisfy me. You don't marry to be alone. Married couples can live together and still be miles apart even though events are still going on. Each time I was discouraged, depressed or saddened my husband would buy me something. All I desired from him was to be close to his heart and given affection and attention. I wanted us to have quality time. I wanted us to give acts of services and gift-giving for the right reasons, not just to appease. It seemed most difficult for him I thought to give himself.

While I didn't go out looking for an affair, I had one, it found me. The enemy of my soul knew where and who to send. The enemy of our souls will assign demonic forces to defeat God's purpose and plan in your life. He will use whomever he can to attack the weaknesses within you. I was unhappy inside, lonely for a deeper relationship with my then spouse. I felt numb to the world and I cried a lot. I took full responsibility for what I did and my role in the demise of my marriage. Sure, there were other factors that contributed to the frailties that were apparent. My ex-husband wasn't totally innocent, but I'm not here to speak for him. I can only speak for myself. So much happened that year and just when you think everything is okay despite the inner pains, it seems a wind of circumstances blew in the wrong direction. A young man walked into my life and swept me away. It took me months to give over to those ungodly behaviors. It wasn't immediate, the enemy to our souls are never immediate. When the foundation in your life is cracked, it starts there, and the rest of the layers are gradually peeled away. You tend to make excuse, and reasons why you should cross that line. You justify your actions and even spiritualize them. The consequences are far more damaging than the pleasure you hope to gain from the act. When it was made known my entire life crashed before my eyes. Destruction and mayhem are the only way I can describe it. I ended-up in severe depression and admitted myself in a mental health facility in up-state Washington for an entire month. I had a nervous breakdown. Extremely close, flesh and blood family members 'betrayed' me. I shared the experience of that affair as it was ending. I knew it wasn't the life I wanted for myself, because I wanted to live a godly life.

They told my then husband. I was exposed to family and friends, on my job, in my church circles, you name it. The avulsion type wound to the soul is a deadly one and serious. You can cause this self-inflicted wound or someone or something else can. Your running, on the move in life, then a yank, a tear to all that belongs to you occurs. WHAT IN GOD'S NAME DO YOU DO NOW?

A song comes to mind, "Be still my soul, the Lord is on your side, wait patiently, the cross of guilt and shame in everything the Lord is on your side." King David did some horrible things. Yet the bible tells us he was the "APPLE OF GOD'S EYE," consequences of sins are inevitable, but in His great love, while we were yet sinners Christ died for us. His grace and mercy are all I can say is what kept me. For 5 years, I suffered inside my soul. I learned through that experience how to WALK & RUN WHILE WOUNDED. I was so very broken. I cried every night to the Lord to please take me home. Death was calling, and I was answering pleading for death to come. The day came when love filled my heart and the Spirit of God overshadow me. It felt like an electric blank had been turn on and gradually warmed my soul. I was so very cold and dead inside myself. Confusion taunted me day and night. I couldn't put 2+2 together to = 4. I didn't know whether I was coming or going most days. I felt abandon and many times were abandoned. BUT LOVE LIFTED ME and FORGIVENESS of SELF RASIED ME.

When you get this type of wound to your soul, I advise you to ask God to forgive you. Forgive yourself and ask others to forgive you. Those who will, will, and those who don't won't, but you've done your part. Some pains will remain and will always be there as a reminder of what happened. It's okay, it can be healthy if you've learned from it. Are you going to be perfect? No. Are the ones that hurt you going to be perfect? No. However, the lesson to be learned here is acceptance, forgiveness, and love no matter what has happened. You can hurt or be hurt with this type of soul wound because life sometimes happen when you least expect. When you're in motion and life seems grand, an 'Avulsion Wound' can occur. Run and not be weary, walk and not faint. You will mount up on wings as eagles and soar again and again. Accept your losses and don't stay in denial. Go through the grieving process, but don't linger in that area for years. It will consume you and life will be over. Love beyond pain is about rising to the occasion to see life has many more chapters other than the one you are currently reading. You can turn that page at any given moment in spite of the pain you feel. It takes courage and faith in Christ to overcome.

PUNCTURE WOUND:

Become Enlighten, See it from a Spiritual Perspective

"A puncture wound is created when a sharp, slender object penetrates the skin and possibly the underlying tissues, depending on the length of the object. In contrast to an incision, a puncture wound is deeper than it is wide. Thus, the entrance site of a puncture wound is generally small and often doesn't cause much superficial bleeding. The surface wound tends to close quickly, but this can cause problems as it may lead to an enclosed pocket of infection. Tetanus is a concern with puncture injuries. Common mechanisms of puncture wounds include stepping on a nail, being bitten by an animal or sustaining a stab wound." (Stephanie Chandler, 2014).

The puncture wound to the soul happens more time than not. Each day, we live around others in close settings and intimate forms. We easily tend to puncture someone's soul. Mistakes are made, things are said out of bounds, and small actions of bad behaviors are committed. We sometimes deliberately hurt others to get their attention or see if they even care. In Proverbs it tells us, "An offended brother is like a contentious city," if you wound a brother, sister, spouse, child or close friend, simply and immediately ask for forgiveness. These small fires can be controlled and remedied, if pride is placed aside and humbleness of heart is the posture taken. Offenses will come, but they need not remain. The quicker you extinguish a fire; the quicker life moves on. Holding any type of fire too long close to your bosom will burn you. You decide if it's worth it or not. Anger left uncheck can and will grow wild. I've learned throughout my years, it's best to resolve it and resolve it quickly. Soulish puncture wounds are something we all can control and recover from. If we care about those around us, and we want to live in peace and harmony as the scriptures instruct us take that step towards healing. We all get tired and weary during our everyday life. Stress and strains of all sorts afflict us. If you puncture someone's soul and you know you did it intentionally, be the big person that you are and make amends. Nobody wins when the soul is punctured. You might feel instant gratification because you saw that person in pain but after while, you will regret it. Fix it, and remember you have a soul too that can be injured.

Other Types of Wounds

There are certainly other types of wounds not included in the 5 categories discussed. Some examples of other types of wounds include: contusion, commonly known as a bruise, thermal, chemical or electrical burn penetrating wound, which extends into an internal organ or body cavity. Skin ulcers, a type of chronic cavitary skin sore. You can research these and see what spiritual correlations God reveal to you.

Warnings and Precautions

Most superficial skin wounds heal within a week or two with simple cleaning and first aid measures. Some wounds, however, require professional medical evaluation and treatment. Seek medical attention if you sustain a deep puncture wound or bite. Medical attention is also recommended for a cut that is large, deep or gaping, or contains debris you cannot rinse away with water. Continued bleeding after 5 to 10 minutes of firm pressure is another indication for professional medical care. Skin wounds due to substantial trauma or that are accompanied by loss of feeling or function in the involved area also require medical care. Drainage of pus, expanding redness around a wound or a fever could indicate a serious skin infection, which requires immediate medical attention. Reviewed and revised by: (Tina M. St. John, M.D., n.d.).

We spoke of 5 types of wounds and other types of wounds. As you're reading now about wounds to the body in your mind, make contrast and correlations about what you are feeling, thinking and compare these wounds to your soul's wounds. Can you see how your body is affected by wounds and how your soul too can be affected? Can you imagine within your mind seeing your soul hurt from pains of others and life in general?

How these wounds can stop you from flowing? It stops healthy blood flow which carries oxygen for your body. It stops your spirit from giving worship and praises to God. It stops your soul from emotional reaching out to love in future relationships. Loving beyond your present pains should not be an event, but a way of life 'SHIT HAPPENS,' you don't know when it's going to happen, why it's happening sometimes, where it will happen but you always and eventually know who caused it to happen. If its important to cleanse a physical wound to the body, it is equally just as important to cleanse a wound to the soul. We are made-up of spirit, soul, and body. According to 1 Thessalonians 5:23 states, "Now may the God of peace Himself sanctify you entirely; and may your spirit, and soul, and body be preserved complete, without blame at the coming of our Lord Jesus Christ" (NASB). Mathew 10:28, "And do not fear those who kill the body but cannot kill the soul. Rather fear him who can destroy both soul and body in hell." Another scripture says, "For the word of God is living and active, sharper than any two-edge sword, piercing to the division of soul and of spirit, of joint and of marrow, and discerning the thoughts and intentions of the heart." (ESV) God gives us the word to saturate our souls in order to cleanse our minds and thoughts. The washing of the word is our ointment, gauze, bandage. Our Lord gives us a way out, we decide whether to apply it.

Jonae Frederick in a 2017 article stated, "When it comes to the care of minor wounds, two types of healing methods exist. The first method, known as moist wound healing, implements moist protective covers to promote healing. Moist healing prevents scabbing, instead promoting the regeneration of new skin cells utilizing the liquid that exudes from the wound. Dry wound healing leaves the wound open to the circulation of fresh air, which helps heal the wound and dry it out through the scabbing process." (2017)

Scabbing is the body's natural way of healing itself. How can we apply scabbing processes to the soul and make this correlation of soul-healings? The word of God states, I am covered over with the robe of righteousness. This righteous of God is the gauze, the moisture or balm given to believers through Christ. Love and forgiveness. When we get into the presence of the Lord and lay in green pastures through meditation His protective coverings promote healing. Without love and forgiveness, the soulish wound is a life naked and bare to spiritual forces that erodes and depletes. Thereby killing the body with visible results. It's been studied and researched from the professional community when a person holds on to unforgiveness internal organs and mental illnesses occurs.

In this next passage read from a scientific perspective present why and how unforgiveness plays a major role in sickness and even death from Everett L. Worthington Jr. (2004).

Perhaps the most basic question to address first is, what is forgiveness? Though most people probably feel they know what forgiveness means, researchers differ about what constitutes forgiveness. I've come to believe that how we define forgiveness usually depends on context. In cases where we hope to forgive a person with whom we do not want a continuing relationship, we usually define forgiveness as reducing or eliminating resentment and motivations toward revenge. My colleagues Michael McCullough Kenneth Rachal, and I have defined forgiveness in close relationships to include more than merely getting rid of the negative.

They further state, the forgiving person becomes less motivated to retaliate against someone who offended him or her and less motivated to remain estranged from that person. Instead, he or she becomes more motivated by feelings of goodwill, despite the offender's hurtful actions. In a close relationship, we hope, forgiveness will not only move us past negative emotions, but move us toward a net positive feeling. It doesn't mean forgetting or pardoning an offense. Unforgiveness, by contrast, seems to be a negative emotional state where an offended person maintains feelings of resentment, hostility, anger, and hatred toward the person who offended him. People can deal with injustices in many ways. They don't have to decide to forgive, and they don't necessarily need to change their emotions. But if they don't change their response in some way, unforgiveness can take its toll on physical, mental, relational, and even spiritual health. By contrast, new research suggests that forgiveness can benefit people's health.

In addition, the researchers state, we wanted to determine whether people's stress levels are related to their ability to forgive a romantic partner. We measured levels of cortisol in the saliva of 39 people who rated their relationship as either terrific or terrible. Cortisol is a hormone that metabolizes fat for quick response to stress (and after the stress ends, deposits the fat back where it is easily accessible around the waist). People with poor (or recently failed) relationships tended to have higher baseline levels of cortisol, and they also scored worse on a test that measures their general willingness to forgive.

When they were asked to think about their relationship, they had more cortisol reactivity that is, their stress hormone jumped. Those jumps in stress were highly correlated with their unforgiving attitudes toward their partner. People with very happy relationships were not without stresses and strains between them. But forgiving their partner's faults seemed to keep their physical stress in the normal range.

(Everett L. Worthington, 2004).

https://greatergood.berkeley.edu/article/item/the_new_sc ience_of_forgiveness

Here are some steps for cleansing physical wounds. Now that you get this spiritual exercise in correlation of physical wounds and soul wounds, as well as cleaning soul wounds, take these steps and use the word of God to heal. Don't forget, you cannot see your soul. You do, however, feel and experience the effects within your soul and body when emotional pain occurs. The body knows the soul is hurt or damage and it too begins an unhealthy downward spiral.

Natural and Spiritual Applications to Recovery

I want to allow your spirit's understanding to be at work here. Take these steps from the physical and begin turning them around in the spirit to work for you. Find scriptures to apply to every action. This will build your faith as you begin searching for answers for your situation. I could find them for you and place them here, but the whole idea of this exercise is to get you moving out of the deepness of the sea of depression, anxiety, frustration, and hopelessness. You must swim, move towards the shores of life and live.

Step 1

Apply pressure to the wound using a clean piece of gauze to stop the initial bleeding. As blood continues to saturate the gauze, add a fresh piece on top of the original piece.

Step 2

Continue to apply pressure for 20 to 30 minutes or until bleeding stops. Remove the gauze afterward and rinse the wound with cool water to remove dirt and debris.

Step 3

Blot the wound dry with a clean, dry piece of gauze. Apply a thin layer of antibiotic ointment to the wounded area using a cotton ball.

Step 4

Cover the wound with a second clean, dry piece of gauze, secured with surgical adhesive tape. The dry gauze will collect any liquid that exudes from the wound, causing a scab to form.

Step 5

Replace the dry gauze covering once a day. Keep the wound covered with the dry gauze until a scab begins to form, which should occur within one to two days.

Step 6

Allow the wound to remain open to the air once the scab forms. All healing will occur under the scabbed-over skin.

<u>Things You'll Need</u>

- Gauze

- Antibiotic ointment

- Surgical adhesive tape

<u>Tips</u>

- Clean the skin around the wounded area with soapy water and a clean, soft cloth if dirt remains after rinsing. However, avoid getting the soap in the wound. (other bad situations, and people which are irritants)

<u>Warnings</u>

Do not apply a wet dressing to the wound. A wet dressing will prevent the wound from drying out. If the wound continues to bleed despite your best efforts to stop it, seek medical attention immediately. A wound that appears red and inflamed after a few days also requires a physician's check to ensure that it is not infected.

(Jonae Fredericks 2017)

https://www.livestrong.com/article/268260-how-to-dry-out-wounds/

I like the tip steps and things you will need to self-heal mentioned in Fredericks example. Gauze = a spiritual mind-set or attitude, Antibiotics = healing scriptures, surgical adhesive tapes = affirmation and meditation of God's word. Keep it clean by the washing of the word through forgiveness and love. It is advised not to allow soap to get in the wound after cleansing. Soap is an irritant and any irritants can cause slow healing and even prevention of that wounds progress. What can we see as some correlations of soaps as well-meaning people around you?

Well-meaning friends, and family members, co-workers, religious people, negative atmosphere, listening to sad songs, songs that remind you of that person, triggers of smell, or taste or sounds, remove them all. God has setup everything for our good. Only open your eyes and be enlighten by them. You will be able to run and walk while wounded.

REFLECTION & NOTES

CHAPTER 6

The Fruit of the Spirit: Love is the Hinge

Love is a verb.

We know that's it's hard to forgive someone that has hurt and disappointed you. Trust me, I feel it more times than not. I write this book out of deep personal pain and loss. Much my fault, some others fault. We all take personal responsibility. Jesus took responsibility for our faults, didn't he? After He took responsibility, because he couldn't swear by no other covenant greater, He then left us a gift. The Holy Spirit is a gift from God. Jesus said, I will go and ask the Father, and He will not leave you comfortless, but will leave you a comforter that will lead and guide you into all truth and knowledge. It's so strange to me, that each time I add to this book, I'm either in emotional pain or about to enter some unforeseen pain or coming out of it.

Being baptized in the Holy Spirit gives us a special insight into the things of God when our spiritual senses are alert. Pain has a way of bringing us into awareness as we are awakened to revelations. We gain

123

insight and truths about ourselves, others, and our surroundings. God speaks and we listen when we are in pain. The fruit of the Spirit are the Lords fruit basket where all believers get to taste the goodness of the Father.

A hinge is defined as: a noun, it's a thing that is: "a movable joint or mechanism on which a door, gate, or lid swing as it opens and closes, or which connects linked" (Wikipedia Dictionary.com).

Doesn't this sound like the workings of the Holy Spirit? Let's discuss the Fruit of the Spirit for a moment, what are the fruit of the Spirt and their functions?

"But the fruit of the Spirit is love, joy, peace, forbearance, kindness, goodness, faithfulness, gentleness and self-control. Against such things there is no law." (Galatians 5:22-23)

"The Greek word translated 'fruit' refers to the natural product of a living thing. Paul used 'fruit' to help us understand the product of the Holy Spirit, who lives inside every believer. The fruit of the Spirit is produced by the Spirit, not by the Christian. The Greek word is singular, showing that 'fruit' is a unified whole, not independent characteristics. The Holy Spirit gives us the power we need to reject those old sinful desires. We can say "no" to sin and accept the "way out" God faithfully provides (1 Corinthians 10:13) by following the Holy Spirit's leading. Holy Spirit constantly works to rid our lives of the *"acts of the sinful nature"* (Gal 5:19) and display *His* fruit instead. Therefore, the presence of the "fruit of the Spirit" is evidence that our character is becoming more like Christ's True, biblical love is a choice, not a feeling. It deliberately expresses itself in loving ways and always seeks the welfare of others. Biblical love is dependent on the giver's character, not emotion. Love chooses to set aside one's own preferences, desires, and sometimes even needs to put the other person first." (Philippians 2:1-3).

(Kathy Howard, 2018)

https://www.crosswalk.com/faith/spiritual-life/what-are-the-fruit-of-the-spirit.html

Love takes the weight of joy, peace, forbearance, kindness, goodness, faithfulness, gentleness and self-control. It moves into action as it stands firm as the hinges of the fruit to swing open and closed like a gate in our lives. You cannot claim to have or walk in any of the fruit without love. The foundation of forgiveness was laid with love when God created all humanity. He sent His only begotten son to die, so that all who believed might be saved. Christ didn't die for perfection, He died despite it. If you're thinking that a person in your life is going to be perfect, then you are truly lost and disillusioned. Grasp this concept, if you or anyone in your life were perfect what would be the purpose of Christ death? If we know that perfection or anything close to it was impossible, then why do we become disappointed. This expectation is a fleshly notion as we build relationships that fail? The Holy Spirt was given to be at work in us and through us to demonstrate and display the heart of God's love. The failure of another is a weakness Christ died for and is forgivable. The ignorant behaviors we all have Christ died for that too. So, why don't we forgive knowing we all are subject to these frailties of life existence?

Love is not an emotion, it's an act that can strike an emotion. I've learned when someone tells me, they

126

love me very much, I stop and think what that word really means in that person's mind? I think about if they know the responsibility of what they've just said to me? I think about does this mean they will love me through my good, bad, and ugly times? Will they forgive me, and look passed all my faults and truly see my needs? I think about, if they knew all I ever done would they still love me? I think about if they saw me naked, without food, and shelter would they provide me with the necessities needed? I think about, if I was emotionally wounded would they sit up all night with me until I fell asleep and still be there in the morning when I awake? I think about the ultimate sacrifice; would they die for my sins and wrongs? You see, so much goes into those 3 words "I LOVE YOU." The fruit of the Spirit rescues all those things mentioned above. Love never turns its back when needed. Love is truly a VERB. It's meant for action, always created to be active. Love doesn't stop because we decide to stop being loving.

Moving on from this I want to discuss just briefly a section on mental illness. I'm entitling this section as:

"BEAUTIFUL CHOAS"

We are still discussing love and forgiveness. But when we think of family, friends, and others that suffer with mental illnesses, do we love them beyond their pains and ours? We tend sometimes to throw love and forgiveness out the window, and the baby out with the bath water, so-to-speak; when caring for people with mental illnesses. Beautiful Chaos deals with people in our lives whose lives are very chaotic. They themselves are beautiful people, but their mental conditions can sometimes cause much emotional pain and cloud our view of them. Jesus dealt with those that primarily were infirmed, sick of the palsy, possessed with demons, and who had mental illnesses. It's funny how we can see every ailment being healed by Jesus during His time here accept for mental illnesses. Churches and religious gatherings have not addressed these issues when a person is suffering with mental conditions. Some evangelist, pastor, or deacon when encountering this population wants to start casting out demons.

The ignorance and lack of knowledge to be skilled to address these issues, keeps them from helping so many people correctly. How long are the body of Christ going to remain ignorant? One of God's gifts to the body of Christ is the discerning of spirits. In 1 John 4:1 states, "Beloved, believe not every spirit, but try the spirit whether they are of God: because many false prophets are gone out into the world." 1 Corinthians 12:8-10 part of that says, "For to one is given by the Spirit the word of wisdom; to another the word of knowledge by the same Spirit." v10, "To another the working of miracles; to another prophecy; to another discerning of spirits; to another divers kinds of tongues; to another the interpretation of tongues." (KJV).

This is not to say that demonic forces are not at play in some form or another, but like any other illness; when we are down a lot of attacks from unseen force jump on the band-wagon. We need to begin to educate ourselves about mental illnesses. People are suffering and many just walk away from family, friends, and others because they feel that person has a lot of personal issues. We label them as mean, angry, crazy with attitudes all the time, or withdrawn, constantly looking or feeling sad and the list goes on and on. Marriages break-up, people leave home all because they cannot understand what's wrong with the person they love. I find that most individuals with mental health issues are beautiful people. They live in a kind of beautiful chaotic world. Often behaviors are misunderstood and lack of energy for any length of time takes away from positive activities with friends and family.

People with mental illnesses suffer greatly, and if you have someone in your life which suffers with any disease that is affecting your relationship seek help for that person. More importantly, seek help for yourself to try and understand your loved one. Don't abandon them, or easily get angry. Try to understand him or her and remain as loving and patient as possible. Affirm your love for them. Research this disease and effects on the brain. Learn the signs that might trigger emotional spirals. Mental illness sufferers are not spooky or people from another planet. Depending on the severity and type of the illness some have become dangerous without medication. GET HELP! However, don't assume that everyone who suffers are dangerous. This stigma must end and only those that encounter it can speak up. Beautiful Chaos in my dubbing as such is to say; people with mental illnesses in their world things sometimes can become chaotic even for them. See the person with eyes of love and a heart of compassion. Jesus loved them and loved healing them from suffering. We may not be able to heal them, but the power of love and medical treatments most certainly can go a long way. Forgive them for what they sometimes can't help. I'm sure if they had a choice, they wouldn't choose this disease upon their lives. Don't run away from them, seek help for them and love them beyond your pain. If you feel you're in danger get help.

There are helps support groups you can reach out to. Do all you can, and when you feel you can no longer assist, then find support. If you feel you must leave that person, do it humanely and not arrogantly or in anger. Leaving any relationship with a bad taste in your mouth ca hold your soul up from moving on.

DESCRIPTION OF CLIICAL DEPRESSION:

Requires a medical diagnosis

The persistent feeling of sadness or loss of interest that characterizes major depression can lead to a range of behavioral and physical symptoms. These may include changes in sleep, appetite, energy level, concentration, daily behavior, or self-esteem. Depression can also be associated with thoughts of suicide.

People may experience:

Mood: anxiety, apathy, general discontent, guilt, hopelessness, loss of interest, loss of interest or pleasure in activities, mood swings, or sadness

Sleep: early awakening, excess sleepiness, insomnia, or restless sleep

Whole body: excessive hunger, fatigue, loss of appetite, or restlessness

Behavioral: agitation, excessive crying, irritability, or social isolation

Cognitive: lack of concentration, slowness in activity, or thoughts of suicide

Weight: weight gain or weight loss

Also, common: poor appetite or repeatedly going over thoughts

Consult a doctor for medical advice

Sources: <u>Mayo Clinic</u> and others

Possible causes include a combination of biological, psychological, and social sources of distress. Increasingly, research suggests these factors may cause changes in brain function, including altered activity of certain neural circuits in the brain. The persistent feeling of sadness or loss of interest that characterizes major depression can lead to a range of behavioral and physical symptoms. These may include changes in sleep, appetite, energy level, concentration, daily behavior, or self-esteem. Depression can also be associated with thoughts of suicide. The mainstay of treatment is usually medication, talk therapy, or a combination of the two. Increasingly, research suggests these treatments may normalize brain changes associated with depression-(Mayo Clinic, 2017)

Mayo Clinic

<u>https://www.gstatic.com/healthricherkp/pdf/clinical_dep ression.pdf</u>

According Christina Gregory (2018) in an article wrote,

"As women, we have many life roles. Mother, wife, employee, friend, healer, caregiver, and the list go on. The complexity of all these roles can cause ups and downs throughout life. Some of these mood changes may be due to life events (e.g., getting in an argument with a friend) or may be due to hormones (e.g., pregnancy, menstrual cycle). In general, after a few days, your emotions tend to level out and you don't feel down in the dumps anymore. But, if you are suffering from depression, your "downs" don't go away after a few days and may interfere with your daily life activities and relationships. This can be a debilitating cycle and can occur due to several causes. Symptoms can last weeks, months, or years and can be intermittent or a one-time occurrence. Depression is almost twice as likely to affect women than men and tends to have different contributing causes in women than it does in men. Contributing factors include reproductive hormones, a differing female response to stress, and social pressures that are unique to a woman's life experiences. Listed below are the different forms of depression most common in women."

Major Depression

Major depression is a severe form of depression where a woman loses her ability to find pleasure in activities once considered enjoyable. In addition, it affects a woman's ability to work, sleep, and eat in normal and effective manners and usually negatively impacts interpersonal and social relationships. With major depression, also known as major depressive disorder, your depressed state may persist for an extended period of time and is often accompanied with low self-esteem.

Postpartum Depression

This is a special form of depression that occurs after the birth of a baby – often referred to as the "baby blues." Typical symptoms of depression begin in the months following birth, while in some women, they can occur while still pregnant.

Persistent Depressive Disorder

Considered a milder form of depression, this is an extended depressed mood that lasts for two years or more. Major depressive episodes (i.e., more severe forms of depression) may still occur during persistent depressive disorder.

Premenstrual Dysphoric Disorder

Depression that is tied to a woman's menstrual cycle. In this form of depression, severe mood swings, anxiety, and negative thoughts present themselves in the week prior to the start of menstruation and dissipate once the menstrual period begins. Depressive symptoms are severe enough to negatively impact interpersonal relationships and interfere with daily activities.

Some of the distinguishing factors in how depression differs between women vs. men include:

- Women feel anxious and scared; men feel guarded

- Women blame themselves for the depression; men blame others

- Women commonly feel sad, worthless, and apathetic when depressed; men tend to feel irritable and angry

- Women are more likely to avoid conflicts when depressed; men are more likely to create conflicts

- Women turn to food and friends to self-medicate; men turn to alcohol, TV, sex, or sports to self-medicate

- Women feel lethargic and nervous; men feel agitated and restless

- Women easily talk about their feelings of self-doubt and despair; men hide feelings of self-doubt and despair-considering it a sign of weakness

In addition to medications and therapy, the self-help techniques below can help improve your mood if you are suffering from depression:

- Don't keep your feelings bottled up – find a support group with people you trust

- Stay engaged in social activities and social functions

- Exercise regularly

- Get enough sleep – 8 hours per night is ideal

- Meditate, try yoga, or practice other relaxation techniques

If you or a loved one are suffering from depression, you are not alone. Seek help for your depressed mood to elevate your quality of life. If you are unsure who to contact, try the following resources:

- Family doctors

- Employee assistance programs

- Mental health centers

- Social agencies

- Mental health specialists (psychiatrists, social workers, mental health counselors)

- Private clinics

- State hospital outpatient clinics

- Health maintenance organizations (**Depression in Women** Types, Causes, Symptoms, and

Treatments Christina Gregory, 2018)

https://www.psycom.net/depression.central.wom

en.html

REFLECTION & NOTES

CHAPTER 7

In my own opinion, I believe women experience emotional pain far differently than men. I will present some empirical data to support my claims, but for now briefly, I will attempt to state it from my perspective. As everyone well knows, women are "emotional creatures" There is not much kept inside, and women are very expressive in articulating how they're feeling. Men, on the other hand, do not express a lot of emotions nor do they articulate pain of any sort very well. The bible states, women are fearfully and wonderfully made. We know how to empty out pain. We might not always do it effectively or correctly, but one thing for sure, it's coming out of us. You never read about women in the bible that were crucified, burned, or boiled for being followers of Christ. I wondered why that is? Men, however, were tortured and put to death as we know from the Apostles Paul's writing. Paul talked about how he was the Chief of sinners for persecuting those that believed in Jesus teachings. Paul spoke about his encounters with suffering. We learn and read about some of the other

Apostle's sufferings. Men absorb emotional pains. They are conditioned and taught to take on anything that hurts them.

Women will use every part of themselves to convey to others and demonstrate what they are feeling. Every gesture using their body limbs are actively moving. Tears streaming and voice tones rise and fall with every spoken word. Facial expressions give way to more descriptive inner emotional despair. Society by enlarge have taught men from the time they are born that crying is a weakness. Statistically, men end up with more heart diseases, and strokes from keeping feelings hidden unexpressed. They are taught not to complain and "suck it up." Even for them expressing certain emotions of hurt are not easily articulated. While it seems, men are initiators of love expressions, they are slow at expressing words of love. With the rise of love songs to express love, some men will try to emulate music lyrics in their behaviors. This can be very damaging if what they are following to be love acts from a love song is false. Their imaginations often are from what they hear. If there is no example such as a Father loving his mother, how does he learn what love is?

Love songs do not teach men to take personal responsibility to act in a concrete and meaningful way. Everything they are being taught to do from a love song is superficial and never addresses the true needs of a woman. This is not to say love songs are useless, they just are not very good teaching tools to help address emotional pains. Love songs are very beautifully expressed by most artists. However, oftentimes, they do not meet deeper emotional pains in validating and understanding personal inner needs. It's a FAKE REALITY played out in a REAL-LIFE stage.

Emotional pains for females are a very serious matter, one that should not be taken lightly. These pains will affect and create health issues. If she's pregnant, it will affect the unborn child's emotional well-being. Many men are not equipped to handle or address the emotional needs of women. Who taught them? Where did they learn it? Where are they obtaining information from? Gaining knowledge of both male and female's emotional pains can prevent a whole lot of unnecessary misplaced, and displaced words, actions, and bad behaviors. I suggest before intimately bonding, go to Christian counseling and buy some great books on relationships. I would ask these same questions to the women as well. Do you understand the emotional needs of a man's pains? Or do you put them down like society with the same expectations of not showing emotional pains?

Men are problem-solvers, they want to fix everything instead of just listening. They tend to want to work through their emotional pains themselves. If they have a good friend to talk with, they will share emotions of sort. However, wouldn't it be better if their spouse, girlfriend could hear their hearts and respond accordingly or appropriately? It is possible, but again studying the emotions of a man just like a woman is something one must take interest in doing. Sometimes, women think men have the ability to love other women beyond their pains. What they do is much like self-medicating. They cover-up. They once again hide those emotional pains and try to make a go with another relationship. Those relationships usual end-up in failures because they didn't acknowledge their pains. Men don't admit what's wrong or what went wrong in an honest way (pride).

Men just go for what they know. Women might follow these same behaviors, but for her the woman will withdraw when severely hurt. She will take years to recover from emotional pains. Recovery is not so immediate. Love beyond pain, so you can live again teaches from a biblical perspective of overcoming emotional hurts. Forgiveness and love are the foundational principles first and above all else. Forgiving everything not just parts is the second thing. Forgiving self is the primary course of action. Seeking to move towards self-affirmation, acts of serving, giving, touching, spending quality time with who you are is healthy. One cannot as a believer, be sustained for any length of time when hurt if they are not moving in the love of God's law. The fruit of the Spirit is the helper, the guide, and the comforter. Jesus told His disciples, when I leave you, I will not leave you comfortless. Jesus was saying, I will not leave you without my love. His love does not hurt, and love does not cause pain. Love being an action word can invoke an emotion but is not an emotion. This is the mistake we make with love.

The act of love strikes through what we are born with within us (our souls). Meaning, when Jesus died on the cross it was an act of great love. His actions displayed loving through giving. However, when the people saw what had been done to him and what He was doing for them, some had emotional responses, and some did not. But to that end, love actions were on display and was evident. Loves design and purpose is to invoke a human response. Where there is no response to love's actions, there's little inner emotional connections to the act. So, when a person says, "You don't love me," what is really being convey and not correctly articulated is "you've done nothing or you're not doing anything to invoke an emotional response from my human need. Or when a person says, "I don't love you anymore," what he or she is truly stating is, "I will not do anything more in any way, shape or form of demonstrating acts of love towards you." So, since love is an action word, simply put the person stops their actions to discontinue any emotional reactions.

We all have the ability to receive and reciprocate feelings of emotions. What we do with love is create acts that will invoke human loving responses. However, we also have an ability to strike up certain bad emotions and move towards applying actions that not so lovely. For example, you could be thinking of children that are less fortunate in another country. As you're having these thoughts of empathy or sympathy, you move to act in such a way as to implement acts of love through kindness by giving. The love acts you implement may be to give to an organization that helps with these crises. Or you might decide to adopt or send funding or clothing to missionary organizations. You might even go to such foreign countries and serve. This is your service of love, your acts. Everything you see, feel, smell and touch within God's world is His love on display. The word of God tells us, in John 10:10, Jesus said, "The thief cometh not, but for to steal, and kill, and destroy: I am come that you might have life and that you might have it more abundantly." (KJV) That word 'LIFE' is God's love. Love gives life from beginning to end, from conception until death. It moves within the process of time and space by way of cycles. Nothing ever stays the same, love is constantly on the go. The 'abundant' aspect of love is a renewing or transformation from natural experiences of love into a deeper enlightenment of the spiritual love of God.

God never intended for a woman to make a man happy. Nor did he intend for her to make him or their children happy. One writer put it this way, "Skeptics have often asked whether a person who uses cocaine every day is "happy." If feeling good all the time were our only requirement, then the answer would be "yes." However, recent research suggests that an even-keeled mood is more psychologically healthy than a mood in which you achieve great heights of happiness regularly after all, what goes up must come down. Furthermore, when you ask people what makes their lives worth living, they rarely say anything about their mood. They are more likely to cite things that they find meaningful, such as their work or relationships. Recent research even suggests that if you focus too much on trying to feel good all the time, you'll undermine your ability to feel good at all in other words, no amount of feeling good will be satisfying to you, since what you expect (all the time) isn't physically possible for most people. The research suggests that happiness is a combination of how satisfied you are with your life (for example, finding meaning in your work) and how good you feel on a day-to-day basis. Both are relatively stable that is, our life changes, our mood fluctuates, but our general happiness is more genetically determined than anything else. The good news is, with consistent effort, this can be offset.

(Acacia Parks, Ph.D., 2018 Assistant Professor of Psychology at Hiram College).

https://www.happify.com/hd/what-is-happiness-anyway/

We have allowed society to trick us into thinking that our happiness lies between what another human-being does. If it were within our power to sustain happiness for another, then God would have equipped us with such powers. But, He didn't. If those powers of happiness were given to us there would be no pain, no hurt, no sorrows, no divorces, no relationship disasters, none of that. Everyone would be as the writer stated feeling good every day in better words 'high on cocaine' never to come down. We can only find meaning in our lives, purpose and direction of heart in what brings us some contentment or comfort.

We were not designed to live forever in this world. Our original design through Adam and Eve failed. So, we must except and embrace this life by creating quote unquote 'happiness' for self. Let others that want to join in celebrate with you. If not, then still be happy within self. Every day is not going to be a happy one. I have less happy days than what I should have. But whose fault is that? Who should I blame huh? At any moment I can create a moment of contentment or comfort that can bring me some level of happiness. I have suffered with depression and anxiety for most of my life. But when I choose to become creative at those down moments, I find comfort and contentment. My mood then changes which is hard to do, but not impossible. Some days it wins out, and I lay down and take a nap. Other times, I struggle to regain myself. However, I'm still here God is on my side. I've given up on the ideas that one of my duties as a woman is trying to make a man or anyone happy. That is the individual's job alone. Women stop trying to make men happy, men stop trying to make her happy. Instead, let them be free to find their own happiness. And, I should say, your happiness should never cost someone else's misery. If we learn to discuss our feelings and be open to the interpretations of each other's feelings, we can really set ourselves free.

Men experience emotional pains too. I think sometimes women don't think in terms of men having emotional pains. A man could be hurting for years and never say a thing about it. He will carry it or display it in other ways. The bible tells us that we are to be 'a help meets.' Love acts in such a way as to fully wanting to help meet whatever needs to be met. If you have it within your power or ability to meet it, then allow your acts of service towards him meet what's most important to him. Love is not selfish, it's not puffed-up, does not want its own way, but love is kind. When you can love beyond your own pains, you are being very kind indeed.

Ask your man these questions: Honey, is anything hurting you today? Is there anything I can get you or do for you? Would you like to talk about it? Can we talk about it? Or say sweetheart, "I know something is weighing on you, and I don't know what it is, but let me rub your neck, your feet, or even better let me give you a body massage to comfort you." You don't have to express it in this way, but you get my point. You might not ever be able to ease his emotional pains, but you sure can make him relaxed and forget it if just only for a moment. Acts of service can help ease anyone's emotional pains. If we paid more attention to one another, we would be amazed at the affects. Pay attention, give notice to things he or she wouldn't think you cared about. Touch him or her when your close by don't just pass by. Reach out your hand of love.

According to Dr. Melody M. McCloud in an article in Psychology Today (2018) wrote, "I think it's fair to say that we women are generally perceived to be the more emotional sex, the ones to more readily express our pain. Some say we even have more emotional intelligence. But just as men can experience physical maladies usually attributed to women, they likewise can and do experience emotional maladies because of women. Just as their breasts are not as prominent or readily visible, many men's emotions and pains may not be prominently displayed. Men often will hide their emotions. They also are often reluctant to seek counseling. Perhaps it's fear of revealing their emotions, uncertainty, bravado, stubbornness or not wanting to appear weak. As a woman, I admit I don't always "get it," but as a doctor who listens carefully to those seeking my counsel, I can say men do have feelings. They can experience intense pain in a relationship. They do hurt in their heart, and many suffer in private for extended periods of time. Thus, it's important for women to be considerate of their man's feelings, just as we expect they will be considerate and understanding of ours" (Men Feel Pain, Too: Despite their pain, men often hide emotions, resist counseling,

Dr. Melody McCloud, April 9, 2011

https://www.psychologytoday.com/us/blog/black-womens-health-and-happiness

REFLECTION & NOTES

CHAPTER 8

So many times, we hang onto what we define love to be. We emotionally invest our time, energy, and resources towards another thinking its love. The ideas of letting go of what you might think love was is crucially painful. Then again, it might be love for you, but something entirely different for your partner. I think to remain on the safe-side a question should be asking: "WHAT DOES LOVE MEAN TO YOU?" Each time I've given my life over to share with a man, love was never what we each thought it meant towards the other. As I reflect over the years that I gave to marriages, and lovers in my truest definition of what I thought love was or should have been, it never was love. To me, it seems I lived a very lonely life. Looking for a certain kind of love that never existed in any of the men that proclaimed their love for me. And maybe too, I couldn't define it for myself. What were their motives? For some reason, women have a fairy tale imagination. We see love through a lens that was created within us ever since we were little girls.

If we were lucky, our fathers called us "his little princess" mine never called me anything like that. However, in 2009, I was taking a trip to Aruba and needed my birth certificate. I sent to the township where I was born and requested it. Faye Thomasina Venerable is what I thought my name was all my life. I thought my parents had come up with a girlish name that was close to my father's name as possible. I received a call from that township telling me, "We do not have a certificate under that name." To my surprise I said, "Oh really, why is that? They didn't know. However, they said, "We do have a Faye Thomas Venerable." I became very excited as to why my middle name was directly spelled just as my fathers. I called my elder brother who had called me Faye Thomas all my life. I just thought he was cutting it short for "Thomasina," he told me that Faye Thomas Venerable was my real name. You might ask, what does this have to do with letting go of what a person thought was love? I bring it up because it only occurred to me that my father loved me enough to give me his name. Generally, the boy gets his father's first name as junior, but for some reason my dad crowned me with his birth name. I thought my dad didn't love me at all. My father never expressed love but naming me Thomas was an expression of his love I will always bear. I thought his way of loving me was to provide for me only, but he took it a step further.

The word of God tells us in John 3:16, "For God so loved the world that He gave His only begotten son," when Christ died those of us that accepted His love and believed were sealed by the Holy Spirit. The bible tells us further that God gave us a name not even the angles can sing. A name above all names, he called us His righteousness, His beloved children. Letting go of what you think is love might require a name change. You may have to let go of the ideological fantasies embedded in your mind from many well-meaning channels that were false. We falsify love certain ones because of our emotional needs to be loved. We are quick to label the simple actions of another as being love. We get so thirsty to be held, touched, looked upon, spoken to; embracing any resemblances of what appears to be love. I did this most of my life. I must own up to it, and say it failed every time. The pain of letting go what I thought was love allowed me to feel real pain in my heart. A false action can cause a real reaction. I cannot restore the years I've lost searching for true love. I can only pick-up from what's left and pray that I have a better understanding. My guide moving forward is what the bible tells us is true love.

In 1 Corinthians 13: 4-7 it says, "Love is patient, love is kind. It does not envy, it does not boast, it is not proud. 5 It does not dishonor others, it is not self-seeking, it is not easily angered, it keeps no record of wrongs. 6 Love does not delight in evil but rejoices with the truth. 7 It always protects, always trusts, always hopes, always perseveres." (NIV). If love is not functionally and consistently operating in this manner, it's not loves. You must let what you thought was loving to be put off from you. When a spouse or partner can walk away, you can match his or her actions to 1 Corinthians 13 standards. Was the person patient, kind, non-envious, not boastful, not prideful, he or she did not dishonor you or others, did not seek for self-interest, was not easily provoked, did not exchange tit-for-tat, did not delight in your pain, but rejoiced with you in truth? I want to be clear and say, I'm writing from a place of experiences. I've been hurt, and

I've hurt others as well. This not only applies to a spouse or partner, but to children, and other family members and friends. We waste a lot of time trying to function in dysfunctional relationships because we want to fix it. Or we are afraid of letting go and allowing God to fix it. We don't want to let go of what's obvious broken and irreparable we cling to it likes it's the end of the world. I'm not talking to couples that truly love each other and live by the principles of 1 Corinthians 13, but those of us that keep trying to live by a set of principles that are not working and clearly are false. We keep trying to apply the same old applications expecting different results. When are we going to stop it?

"Time stands still for no man," shattered dreams and wounded hearts live until they die. Love beyond your pains is a very difficult road to travel, but at least you've decided to travel it. This is the walking while wounded road, you feel the hurt and disappointments, but you keep moving. Going back a few chapters, I said I would mention a relationship I was in for a year. Some might say, since it was an online relationship it really doesn't count as being real. I beg to differ. However, the crazy part of it, I never saw or heard this man voice until a year later. I won't go into any details except to say, I gave a whole lot for this invisible man. It's too much to even explain in these writings. This man took my heart and soul and my money for an entire year. He held it through lies, deceit, and betrayal. You might ask how? I was vulnerable to the same needs and desires I spoke of a few lines ago. The need to be in relationship because I was profoundly lonely. The need to belong to someone. Loneliness drives us to do things we might not would otherwise do. This man stole someone else's profile. A very world-wide known figure. I never heard of this man I began this relationship with. If I called his name now many of you would know him. But anyway, this person I was conversing with stole the identity and played it to the fullest. Blinded by my own pain, sadness, and desire for love I believed in him.

Talk about being blind, I was blind-sided and caught-up in a fantasy world of my own. I rationalized it by thinking, at least I'm not alone and I have someone to talk too. I paid a heavy price for false love and letting go wasn't going to be easy. After this man revealed himself to me, he then asked for forgiveness. Of course, I forgave him, prayed with him, but the fantasy wasn't over. Due to what I thought was love from the heart, I continued conversating with him. At least now I have face with a real name belonging to a real person. I didn't feel crazy anymore about my thoughts that I'm being scammed because I really was. I allowed my mind to trick and play games with my emotions. We continued talking for 2 more months face-time. I was angry yes, but I was in love too. In love, what a word. It wasn't love because it didn't measure up to 1 Corinthians 13: 4-7. I finally let go, and it hurt terribly. False actions, real reactions. When you give your soul away even into a fantasy world, it's not going to be so easy to escape unscarred. Remember, in Chapter 5, we discussed different types of wounds? Mine was the worse one of all. However, I broke free and continue to walk and run though I wounded.

God created us and fashioned us in such a way that our nourishment for life is connected to life. "It is not good that man should be alone for I will make a help meet for him." (KJV) You never see a flower standing alone, a bird flying alone, a tree growing alone, the animals born from its own nature thriving or surviving alone. You never see a fish swimming alone, or the stars and planets within the universe hanging alone. Everything that lives and move belongs to a community of like-kind. If you see any of these alone, it wasn't Gods doings, but something mankind altered in. Love is about community, coexisting, relating to that which is equal to itself. Love is about embracing and exploring something outside of yourself and accepting it as a creation design by God. I'm not talking about the perversion of what sin has done, but the love of what God created from the beginning. We were born into sin, nothing will ever change that. However, when we accept Christ, we see life and others how God intended "whole". The worse thing I feel most times is loneliness and abandonment by those I love and have loved. I struggle every day to make sense of my own life finding no comfort in the knowledge that even though I'm in God's hands, I don't want to be alone.

What do we have to truly guide us accept the word of God and the Holy Spirit? Yes, God gave us our natural senses and abilities, but there is something far greater than that which we see, feel, hear and touch. A longing to be in another space in time knowing the pure love of God. As God would have it, we are here on this earth. For as long as He says so, here we must stay. I've had to let go of lost relationships that failed. But true love never fails because 1 John 4:7-8 stated, "Beloved let us love one another for love is God and everyone that loveth is born of God and knows God. He that loveth not, knoweth not God for God is love." (KJV) So, just as we can love, we can choose not to love, but if we don't love, then we don't know God. Out of all the encounters you can possibly think of, ask yourself if you loved by Gods rule of law about love? Let go of the false notions and misconceptions of what you thought love was supposed to be like. Each time I found myself hurt by a man I was in love with, I measured his love for me by my own feelings and standards of love. He had a different standard or understanding than I did. Therefore, it was impossible for me to accept why he hurt me. Some might say, love is an intense deep emotional feeling. Well, if love is a 'intense deep emotional feeling' that means sometimes we might love and other times we might not. Love is not a feeling. Love is action taken towards another that is encapsulated with kindness, temperance, self-control, meekness, and gentleness. Love invokes these emotions. Love is an ignitor. Love is forever and always moving. Love never seeks its way, is not proud or boastful. Love don't hurt, people do.

If I had been more patient, kind, tolerant, understanding, honest, and open I would still be married to my former husband I believe. I really didn't get the enlighten understanding of love until 5 years after my husband left. Love is not blind, we are. Love sees so clearly and understands so profoundly, that even in our stupid mistakes love still loves us. Why is it so hard for us to let go? When a blind person cannot see their way and has never been skilled at or trained to navigate in the dark; that person will stumble and fall every time. Being afraid of the dark he or she clings to that which is comfortable or safe. We do relationships the same way. We are afraid to let go even though we know it's not love. Being blind to truth, keeps you from the light of true love. Truth sets you free because truth is love, and love is truth. So, the next time you are blinded to "love" realize that it never was love. Love is not blind nor does blind you or keep you in the dark. Love is a light and is the life force of God and will always lead you in the right direction. This we must keep reminding ourselves of, so we can be free from what we thought was love. Dark love is a form of a false imitation of God's truth or laws of love. Dark love is a blinding so-called love that keeps us from following truth. When we succumb to the will of the flesh and the desires of the mind and of the flesh, we fall into dark love. The laws of God's love convict us of sin and leads us towards Christ not away from Him.

The Law was given so that we may be convicted of sin ("by the Law is the knowledge of sin;") to lead us to Christ; and to be the rule for the believer's life. While Christians are not under the Law, as far as punishment and condemnation is concerned, they are enormous, under the Law of Christ, whom they love and desire to serve. And they serve Him best who obey Him in all His will: "Whosoever therefore shall break one of these least commandments, and teach men so, he shall be called the least in the kingdom of heaven..." (Matthew 5:18). "He that has my commandments and keeps them he it is that

loves   me...''-   (Truth   for   Today
http://www.tecmalta.org/tft186.htm).

1 John 1:5-6 (ESV)

[5] This is the message we have heard from him and proclaim to you, that God is light, and in him is no darkness at all. [6] If we say we have fellowship with him while we walk in darkness, we lie and do not practice the truth.

1 John 2:9-11 (ESV)

[9] Whoever says he is in the light and hates his brother is still in darkness. [10] Whoever loves his brother abides in the light, and in him there is no cause for stumbling. [11] But whoever hates his brother is in the darkness and walks in the darkness, and does not know where he is going, because the darkness has blinded his eyes.

Dark love "false love" keeps us in emotional turmoil and confusion about life. The works of the flesh as stated in **Ephesians 5.**

Walk in Love

5 Therefore be imitators of God, as beloved children. [2] And walk in love, as Christ loved us and gave himself up for us, a fragrant offering and sacrifice to God.

[3] But sexual immorality and all impurity or covetousness must not even be named among you, as is proper among saints. [4] Let there be no filthiness nor foolish talk nor crude joking, which are out of place, but instead let there be thanksgiving. [5] For you may be sure of this, that everyone who is sexually immoral or impure, or who is covetous (that is, an idolater), has no inheritance in the kingdom of Christ and God. [6] Let no one deceive you with empty words, for because of these things the wrath of God comes upon the sons of disobedience. [7] Therefore do not become partners with them; [8] for at one time you were darkness, but now you are light in the Lord. Walk as children of light [9] (for the fruit of light is found in all that is good and right and true), [10] and try to discern what is pleasing to the Lord. [11] Take no part in the unfruitful works of darkness, but instead expose them. [12] For it is shameful even to speak of the things that they do in secret. [13] But

when anything is exposed by the light, it becomes visible, [14] for anything that becomes visible is light.

https://www.biblegateway.com/passage/?search=Ephesians+5&version=ESV

The example of letting go what you thought was love and embracing what true love can be is found in Ephesians 5

Wives and Husbands

[22] Wives submit to your own husbands, as to the Lord. [23] For the husband is the head of the wife even as Christ is the head of the church, his body, and is himself its Savior. [24] Now as the church submits to Christ, so also wives should submit in everything to their husbands.

[25] Husbands, love your wives, as Christ loved the church and gave himself up for her, [26] that he might sanctify her, having cleansed her by the washing of water with the word, [27] so that he might present the church to himself in splendor, without spot or wrinkle or any such thing, that she might be holy and without blemish.[a] [28] In the same way husbands should love their wives as their own

bodies. He who loves his wife loves himself. [29] For no one ever hated his own flesh, but nourishes and cherishes it, just as Christ does the church, [30] because we are members of his body. [31] "Therefore a man shall leave his father and mother and hold fast to his wife, and the two shall become one flesh."[32] This mystery is profound, and I am saying that it refers to Christ and the church. [33] However, let each one of you love his wife as himself, and let the wife see that she respects her husband.

(https://www.biblegateway.com/passage/?search=Ephesi ans+5&version=ESV).

Let's take a closer look at this description of love between a husband and wife as a reflection of the church and Christ.

Wives submit to your own husbands as to the Lord: the word submit within the content of these ascriptions has created a cloud of dark suspicion on what women are asked to do. To submit means to: accept or yield to a superior force or to the authority or will of another person. If women saw their spouses as a superior force in the order or sense of where God placed the man as stated in 1 Cor, 11:3. But I would have you know, that the head of every man is Christ; and the head of the woman is the man; and the head of Christ is God; women would not feel threaten or inferior to the order of God's command. But dark love causes women to believe that they are to have authority over the man in every way that threatens their womanhood. In the eyes of God, we are equal to the beloved in our inheritance, and place in heavenly places in Christ Jesus. Furthermore, to keep earthly order in a natural sense, the woman takes the position as the weaker vessel for peace and harmony sake. The scripture says, to your own husband. This is especially necessary to state because women can be easily swayed. Not only that it gives continual lead to the man's guidance. It does not state whether the man should be first a follower of Christ, but it does state the order of God as found in verse 23. The husband is the head of the wife even as Christ is the head of the church. This is a position not a condition. A place of honor and respect, a place of preservation and protection. A place of strength that encompasses the safety of the family.

Christ is the head of the church, his body, and is himself its Savior: a man embraces his position within the home as being the watchmen, protector, lifeguard of all that belongs within his care. Christ loved us to death literally. If wives are called to submit to their husbands in everything, husbands are called to submit to God in everything including how they love their wives. Christ loved the church and gave himself up for her, [26] that he might sanctify her, having cleansed her by the washing of water with the word, [27] so that he might present the church to himself in splendor, without spot or wrinkle or any such thing, that she might be holy and without blemish: Dark love or false love does not make sacrifices because its selfish. Christ love sanctifies "to set apart to a sacred purpose" the next part of that scripture says, "having cleansed her" meaning the church the body of Christ is already made clean and forgiven of sin by the washing of water coupled with the word. The blood of Christ has already washed us coupled with His word, "by grace are ye saved not of works lest any man should boast" this and many other scriptures that speaks to our salvation demonstrates our justification. Christ justifies us as we are now glorified "so that he might present the church to Himself in splendor, without spot of wrinkle or any such thing. So, now we are holy and without blemish. This is the law of God's love in the light of truth that we should be called the children of God.

Dark love will not make any such sacrifices. Therefore, the word of God tells husbands to love your wives even as Christ loved the church and gave His life for it. The world deceives us into believing a lie and a false narrative of what love is. When a man tells you he loves you what exactly is he really saying? As previous noted in 1 Cor 13:4-7, "Love is patient, love is kind. It does not envy, it does not boast, it is not proud. [5] It does not dishonor others, it is not self-seeking, it is not easily angered, it keeps no record of wrongs. [6] Love does not delight in evil but rejoices with the truth. [7] It always protects, always trusts, always hopes, always perseveres." (NIV). If a man's love is not in line with the love of Christ, it's dark love a "false love" a fleshly love that is not sustainable. Letting go of what you were conditioned to believe was love is easier said than done. Because it means to reevaluate, recondition, and redefine a system or set of immoral, ungodly beliefs given or instill in the mind and adopted through the flesh throughout the years.

Only the Spirit of truth will set you free from it. It's hard to let go of a lie to embrace a truth. Pain is something we all try to avoid at all cost. Love beyond the pains of hurt, lies, deceit, and comfort of the flesh is a high price to pay, but indeed a valuable one. Love, true love makes those hard choices not to be comforted by dark love that keeps us blinded to truth. Love bares the scares and pains of truth so that in the long run we are saved, we are safe from sure death. We can choose to embrace death or live in light. It's all up to that one thing we all have as human-beings, "free will" Walking and running out the course of life while we are wounded from this life takes courage. Not only courage, but a made-up mind to do the will of God. Loving someone beyond emotional pain can bring you down to a slow pace in your life. However, if you just "keep it moving" you will be alright. It's when we stop, we give up hope, we stop having faith in believing in a brighter day, or that our change will come, is when all is lost. I have many of these days, but something inside me won't let me give up. That something I would like to believe is the Holy Spirit of God within me. For this race is not given to the swift, nor to the strong, but to those that endure to the end."

REFLECTION & NOTES

Chapter 9

We identify personality, intellect, will, and emotions as the soul of who we are. The bible tells us we are body, soul, and spirit in the following scriptures listed below, we can see the word of God explanation of the dichotomy of the human condition. **1 Thessalonians 5:23** - And the very God of peace sanctify you wholly; and [I pray God] your whole spirit and soul and body be preserved blameless unto the coming of our Lord Jesus Christ. **Matthew 10:28** - And fear not them which kill the body, but are not able to kill the soul: but rather fear him which is able to destroy both soul and body in hell. **Ecclesiastes 12:7** - Then shall the dust return to the earth as it was: and the spirit shall return unto God who gave it. **James 2:26** - For as the body without the spirit is dead, so faith without works is dead also. **Hebrews 4:12** - For the word of God [is] quick, and powerful, and sharper than any two-edge sword, piercing even to the dividing asunder of soul and spirit, and of the joints and marrow, and [is] a discerner of the thoughts and intents of the heart.

Genesis 2:7 - And the LORD God formed man [of] the dust of the ground, and breathed into his nostrils the breath of life; and man became a living soul.

We know that our souls are real because it is the make-up of our personality, intellect, will and emotions. The Spirit of God gives us life and that life gives us the ability to live. We function through these processes of God's ordained designs. In Matthew 16:26 it says, "For what is a man profited, if he gains the whole world and forfeits his soul (his personality, intellect, will, emotions), Or what shall a man give in exchange for his soul? (personality, will, intellect, emotions)." Every day, we give up a little part of us for this world's pleasures, goals, and desires. We forfeit our rights as children of God to gain those things that are not eternal. To lose yourself is to deprive yourself from this world, but to gain all that God has for you in the next life after this. The things that destroy the soul can be found in Galatians 5:19 listed below:

Sexual immorality, impurity, lustful pleasures, idolatry, sorcery, hostility, quarreling, jealousy, outburst of anger, selfish ambition, dissension, division, envy, drunkenness, wild parties, the bible states will not inherit the kingdom of God. We must protect our soul much like we protect our bodies from injury. Your soul is real, it's who you are to your very core. An injured soul will only injury another soul if not careful. God has given us the ability to walk and run while wounded, but that comes also with the thought that He can heal us and make us whole as we continue to carry on with life. I wasn't experienced with social media and was quite new to Facebook. Through messenger, someone contacted me named Brandon. Brandon came into my life at a time when I was most vulnerable. I was profoundly alone and desperately wanted friendship and connection with someone anyone as a friend. The same guy spoke of earlier, I didn't provide a name then.

At the time, I didn't know what "Catfish" was. Catfishing is a term used when scammers sit and wait for the right fish, namely a female that's weak and vulnerable to bite the bait. For a year and half, I was that catfish. I can speak about this now because it's my testimony of walking and running while wounded aftermath. I never saw this person, never even spoke to him for the length of time we engaged ourselves in this online love affair. I was just so happy at the time to have someone, to "connect with" Brandon over the months got to know me well. We spoke the same love languages and had such sweet correspondences. I was so satisfied, and so engulfed in our letters and conversations, via messenger, hangouts, and emails. We shared everything. I gave my soul away to Brandon as if he was standing in front of me. As if I saw him every day, several times a day. Little did I know, I was being scammed by a professional former criminal government worker turn rouge.

The same types of criminals Brandon was tracking down for his government was the same type of criminal he became. I developed a very tight soul tie with Brandon. It wasn't one of the flesh, but one of the minds, soul, and I dare say he got into my spirit. Social media is the playground where the innocent is devoured by wolves. The rules of engagement for relationships have shifted dramatically. Caution, if a person cannot or will not show his or her face to you after a few weeks forget about them and move on. After a few months, Brandon began this sob story about being in the military on a special mission. A special mission of what continued to conceal his identity from me ever knowing who he was really and where he was. He said he was in Afghanistan in combat zones. I can't even begin to tell you the extent and the deep seated lies this man told, and I believed every bit of it. I fasted and prayed for his safety and encouraged him every day. His main thing to me was, " I just want to come home." He pleaded and cried to me in his letters to please help him come home. He said his male commander could help him if he gave him sex. He said he was a Christian and didn't want to do it. He said he was an assistant Chaplin there. Wow, if I could write all the details of what this man said it would be unbelievable the deceit and lies, he told. However, Brandon knew he had me. He knew he had my mind, my emotional intellect and my will at his command.

There was nothing I wouldn't do to prove to him how much I loved him. All I can do is shake my head right now as I'm writing this. The shame I felt and still feel at times, unbelievable. An entire year and half of my life gone to a wolf. Even though my spirit was engulfed, the Spirit of God inside me kept telling me this isn't right. I questioned myself, even fasted and prayed for myself to receive clarity. God spoke, but I didn't listen. I was too far gone into this soulish realm, it had to take its course. A year and a half, and thousands of dollars later I was broke and broken. Homeless, and devastated I had nowhere to go, and no one I could tell. I was ashamed, very much ashamed of my life. It wrecked me to the core, and I was desperately trying to live and pick up the pieces. With no home, no car, no money, I moved from place to place living on the streets for 2 weeks in the middle of summer. Nobody will ever know the extent of what happened to me, but I survived.

Brandon contacted me finally by way of video chat. I finally saw the face and heard the voice of the man I loved that not only stole my heart but stole everything of value from me. He posed as this well-known preacher out of Chicago that was in the military. As you might guess, Brandon's real name is not Brandon, nor is his name the same as the preacher's name and profile he stole.

Getting that video chat from who I now know as Johnny, hurt and healed me at the same time. Hurt because I thought how anyone could do this to another human-being? How could a person go so deep into the abyss? When I saw Johnny's face and heard his voice, I broke-down and started crying and my healing began. I cried, and cried, and cried. I was so relieved at first that I truly wasn't crazy. It wasn't my mental illness of depression and anxiety that was causing me to think 'ITS JUST ME.' It truly was the Spirit of God warning me of what was happening. It takes me back to the scripture "Matthew 16:26. It says, for what is a man profited, if he gains the whole world and forfeits his soul?" I wanted to profit having someone to love me, and care about me so much so that I lost my own soul my (personality, intellect, will, and emotions) over to another. Or what will a man give in exchange for his soul? These two questions are the state of mind most of us find ourselves in when we are outside the will and purpose of God. We marry for all the wrong reasons.

This is our fight, this is our earthly battle for now. One day, those of us in Christ Jesus will wake-up to the newness of life eternal where we will "war no more" as the song goes. I can't wait to go home. Your soul is real. Mary mother of Jesus said, "Bless the Lord oh my soul doth magnify the Lord." We can walk and run in this life while we are wounded only, because God strengths us in the inner man to do so. I forgave Johnny and he asked for forgiveness and prayer. I remember asking God to first forgive me for selling my soul over from the call of His Spirit. I wasn't perfect even after all that, but it serves as a reminder that my soul is real, and I can either safeguard it, or give it away. Johnny and I talked still from time to time, but what I give him now during those talks is the word of God's truth. To this day, Johnny tells me of how he is suffering for what he did to me. He's been in jail and out for now. He's suffering, and I just pray for him that God turn him around and use him for the kingdom.

The whole armor of God is for these same purposes. It's to guard your head where the seat of your soul lay; your personality, intellect, will and emotions. The breastplate of righteous is where the spirit is guarded from other spirits. Gird your waist with truth. Your belly your digestive systems feed through here and what you put in your mouth affects the whole body. Your feet shaded with the gospel. You are ready to stand boldly in the presence of God's word. Take the word of God with you and in everything you do. The shield of faith backs you in front and in the rear. The sword cuts down everything that is not of truth that is not of faith and righteousness. Without any of this armor, we are at the mercy of this world and everyone in it. Give peace to your weary soul and rest in the presence of God. All the hurt and pain of what you are experiencing and what you will experience will one day be over. But, for now fight through, pray through, and trust in God through every pain you now feel. YOUR SOUL IS REAL & SO IS GOD!

REFLECTION & NOTES

Chapter 10

God decides I believe who is born into this life, but I think he allows us the choices for our lives. I think when he said, in Jeremiah 29:11, "For I know the plans I have for you," declares the LORD, "plans to prosper you and not to harm you, plans to give you hope and a future," those plans spoken to Jeremiah was specifically spoken to him concerning his path. The Lord was encouraging Jeremiah that better days were coming to Jeremiah. God's plans for Jeremiah were plans to fulfil a greater purpose for the children of Israel. The Lord was informing Jeremiah that he was being chosen and set apart for what was to come. That the false prophets were not of Him. God's plans are not always speedy and immediate as we would like. It took 70 years for the children of Israel to be delivered from the hands of the Babylonians.

When we feel that we are held captive in life circumstances, and it seems like it's going to take a while. However, we can still choose how we love ourselves and others. How we respect ourselves and others, and how we adapt to the emotional circumstances. Shadrach,

Meshack, and Abednego along with Daniel were swept up in this raid by the Babylonians. The unexpected happened, but these boys were confident in their faith in God. Their minds were made up to trust God for their future. If we trust God's plans for our future the decisions of how we will love, respect and deal with emotional pains will cause us to grow spiritually. The plan is still God's. Trusting in God's plans for me was one of the hardest things for me to do. My flesh wants to scream of the loneliness I feel inside. I felt at times, I'm getting older and my situations have not changed. But, within this space of time just like the Hebrew boys, the working of the Holy Spirit moved. I'm sure 70 years seemed like a lifetime to those boys, but they endured it.

The timing of God is so different than the timing of man. Everything with God is accurate and right on time. No matter how late in life we think it is the Lord's plans are yay, nay, and Amen. Remember, He said, "I know the plans is to prosper you. The plan is not to harm you. The plan is to give you hope and a future. While you wait, how will you love, respect and deal with the pains of life? The three Hebrew boys were threatened and thrown into a fiery furnace. Daniel was thrown into the lion's den. Still, they loved God, each other, the people they served and self. The emotional pains of being separated from family and friends I'm sure was hard. All they had ever known was stripped away. Sometimes, we see love in a vacuum. Love is communal, it is shared amongst those that are like-minded for a common good. Love is not an emotion it's a responsibility. It weighs the best interest of others far greater than self. Are you willing to do what's in the best interest of those closes to you?

So many times, when I felt desperate, I wanted to do what was best for me. Early in my life, I convinced myself that I was doing what was in my family's best interest. As I think back now, I feel I was doing what made me feel emotionally better. Love seeks to protect, preserve, and safeguard that which God entrust in your care. I've paid a great price for failing to understand and practice this. Love allows for patience to be developed. Love steps aside and gives the best of what's good to another. Love forgives what hurts is being bared. Love is not puffed-up, it does not act-up. Christ death demonstrates all that love is. If we follow that example, we will come out on top even unto death.

Respect is another area that we are the authors' and finishers within our own lives. Everything we do is a choice. Respecting yourself is an important key to loving yourself. Pain can take us out of joint. Whether it's physical or emotional pain, the natural reaction is to strike back. However, we must remember we are spiritual beings having an earthly experience. When others injure you emotionally it cuts into your soul. Remember, your soul is your personality, intellect, will, and emotions. These four areas at the core of who you are is vulnerable to attack. It is the place where we most dwell. Even though the bible tells us not to do so, we do. This is what makes us human. Scriptures upon scriptures warns of us walking in the flesh. Our bodies only carry out what the mind and the soul tells it too. "WALK NOT AFTER THE FLESH (the soul), BUT AFTER THE SPIRIT AND YOU WILL NOT FULFILL THE WORKS OF THE FLESH AND THE MIND," this is the warning we must strive to heed to daily.

The respect and love you have for your soul should be the same as you would your spirit man. Nobody said this would be easy, but this is our earthly battle until we leave this world. This is the great fight that Satan wages war for against the Spirt of God in you. Satan does not want you to love. Therefore, he does not want you to love self or respect self. Your destruction in a state of sin outside of the will of God is his big target. When there is emotional pain what is the first thing we do? We cry, we hurt, then we react to those emotions. Losing self-respect during an emotional upset is the beginning of falling into an area where the Spirit of God is no longer out front. Some common reactions are those one tends to turn to spoken of in Galatians 5:19, if you go back and read them. These works of the flesh and mind are designated to keep you in emotional turmoil and ultimately kill you.

Because God has given you a freewill, you get to decide how, when, what, and why you act the way you do in a crisis. You are the author of your love, respect, and pains. God is the author and finisher of your faith stated in Hebrews 12:2 which says, in verse 2 "Looking unto Jesus the author and finisher of our faith; who for the joy that was set before him endured the cross, despising the shame and is set down at the right hand of God."(KJV) I love this this verse because he demonstrates this chapter very well. It says, Jesus despised the shame of the cross. In those days, it was a shame to be hung on a cross and crucified. Even though Christ despised the shame of His suffering he withstood it for our sins and endured it. The bible tells us, "For the joy that was set before Him," my God. You can love beyond pain, so you can live again. You can walk and run while the wounds of this life from other inflictions upon you. You can love and respect yourself in the mist of trying times. Jesus is our great example. He paved the way for all that we have and must endure. Therefore, I say, you are the author and finisher of your love, respect and pains.

The loneliness that Jesus faced while he was walking out what he knew was coming. Can you imagine having to know what you are going to be faced with, and you are unable to express or get anyone to feel what you are feeling? I'm sure many have experienced it. The worse thing I've ever felt was the profound loneliness. I mean this in every sense of the word. For Jesus, the cross was physically, painful. However, I think the emotional turmoil leading up to the beatings, and ultimate death was so deep beyond description yes. But the bible tells us Jesus prayed to the Father until he sweated blood. He was so overwhelmed emotionally within his soul. It is there in our souls where decision is determined. It's in our souls where we make or break ourselves into who we are and what we will become.

The emotional pains you endure is what takes you to the next level of your destination. If you can hold on and hold out to the sufferings of the crosses you must bear; you will see yourself soar. "Jesus, who for the joy that was set before him endure his cross" GLORY TO GOD! Your victory is in your endurance and your endurance is tied to your destiny. "God kept me lonely, only to keep me exclusive." (TD Jakes) If you're in a place in your life where you want to lose love and respect yourself, I employ, admonish, and encourage you to hold on to your faith. The soul of you is a natural and predictable response as a human. But the spirit man is always their ready and available to override him.

Discipline in times of great troubles with the leading and guiding of the Holy Spirit is your master key.

The battle is not yours alone, but it's the Lords. All things work in accordance to God's holy will and purpose in your life. You are not alone. The soul of you would have you think you are, but not so. Peace comes when storms are raging. You can feel at peace when there's no storms, but where is peace in the mist of your storms? Jesus told the winds and waves to be still. He wasn't telling peace to be still. He kind of said it in this way "winds, waves, I want peace, so be still" in your emotional pains tell your soul to be still in the presents of God. Pain is something to contend with, it is especially difficult as it stirs within your emotions. Emotional pains trigger physical pains. When your soul is sick your body reacts. When you don't stop emotional pains in its tracks after a time of grieving, it will take over and rule every decision in your life. This is where many of us find ourselves caught up for years making poor choices. We become ensnared in a web of inescapable turmoil. It is here where people commit suicide, kill others, commit all kind of atrocities against another.

194

You are the author and finisher of your pains. You can decide to ask God for healing and walk it out, or you can handle it alone and hope that you make it out. While I was going through my divorce, I attended a church group healing session. I saw so many women there with all kinds of hurt and emotional pains. One woman that came into the session was about 60 or so. This woman for some reason to me looked like my mother even though she was white. I noticed as she tried to share her story, the emotional pain was evident on her face. She reached out for help as best she could, but her pains were too great for her to bear. On our next meeting, we were told she killed herself by running her car off a bridge into the over pass of a lake. Prior to this news, I saw the pictures and the story that broke on the evening news. They showed her slumped over the wheel of her car as they dragged in from the water. Little did I know at the time it was this very same woman. To this day, I ask myself if I could have said or did something to show compassion towards her.

Many times, we are so caught up in our own griefs and sorrows, we can't see the person next to us hurting just as bad, if not more so. At least my husband was still alive after the divorce, but this woman's husband died. She felt all alone and took her life. Emotional pains will rob you of your life. However, you are the author and finisher of your pains. You get to decide whether you will get help and ask God to heal and deliver you from them. There is nothing shameful about a Christian seeking counseling even from someone that is not saved. If he or she is a professional therapist licensed to practice this profession, they are more than qualified. If they are a Christian all the better. They can then couple your sessions with spiritual insight.

Why do we feel emotional pain?

When we feel heartache; for example, we are experiencing a blend of emotional stress and the stress-induced sensations in our chest, muscle tightness, increased heart rate, abnormal stomach activity and shortness of breath. Heartache is not the only way emotional and physical pain intersect in our brain. But how do emotions trigger physical sensations? "Scientists do not know, but recently pain researchers uncovered a possible pathway from mind to body. According to a 2009 study from the University of Arizona and the University of Maryland, activity in a brain region that regulates emotional reactions called the anterior cingulate cortex helps to explain how an emotional insult can trigger a biological cascade. During a particularly stressful experience, the anterior cingulate cortex may respond by increasing the activity of the vagus nerve— the nerve that starts in the brain stem and connects to the neck, chest and abdomen. When the vagus nerve is overstimulated, it can cause pain and nausea"-

https://www.scientificamerican.com/article/what-causes-chest-pains/

How do you heal emotional pains?

According to Dr. Mercola

Emotional pain often exacts a greater toll on your quality of life than physical pain. The stress and negative emotions associated with any trying event can even lead to physical pain and disease.

In fact, emotional stress is linked to health problems including chronic inflammation, lowered immune function, increased blood pressure, altered brain chemistry, increased tumor growth and more.

Of course, emotional pain can be so severe that it interferes with your ability to enjoy life and, in extreme cases, may even make you question whether your life is worth living.

Tips for Healing Emotional Pain

As the featured article reported, Guy Winch, author of *Emotional First Aid: Practical Strategies for Treating Failure, Rejection, Guilt and Other Everyday Psychological Injuries*, recently shared five tips for healing your emotional pain.

Let Go of Rejection

Rejection activates the same pathways in your brain as physical pain, which is one reason why it hurts so much. The feeling of rejection toys with your innate need to belong and is so distressing that it interferes with your ability to think, recall memories and make decisions. The sooner you let go of painful rejections, the better off your mental health will be.

Avoid Ruminating

When you ruminate, or brood, over a past hurt, the memories you replay in your mind only become increasingly distressing and cause more anger – without providing any new insights. In other words, while reflecting on a painful event can help you to reach an understanding or closure about it, ruminating simply increases your stress levels and can be addictive.

Ruminating on a stressful incident can also increase your levels of C-reactive protein, a marker of inflammation in your body linked to cardiovascular disease.[1]

Turn Failure into Something Positive

If you allow yourself to feel helpless after a failure or blame it on your lack of ability or bad luck, it's likely to lower your self-esteem. Blaming a failure on specific factors within your control, such as planning and execution, is likely to be less damaging, but even better is focusing on ways you can improve and be better informed or prepared, so you can succeed next time (and try again, so there is a next time).

Make Sure Guilt Remains a Useful Emotion

Guilt can be beneficial in that it can stop you from doing something that may harm another person (making it a strong "relationship protector"). But guilt that lingers or is excessive can impair your ability to focus and enjoy life.

If you still feel guilty after apologizing for a wrongdoing, be sure you have expressed empathy toward them and conveyed that you understand how your actions impacted them. This will likely lead to authentic forgiveness and relief of your guilty feelings.

Use Self-Affirmations if You Have Low Self-Esteem

While *positive* affirmations are excellent tools for emotional health, if they fall outside the boundaries of your beliefs, they may be ineffective. This may be the case for people with low self-esteem, for whom *self-*affirmations may be more useful. Self-affirmations, such as "I have a great work ethic," can help to reinforce positive qualities you believe you have, as can making a list of your best qualities.

https://articles.mercola.com/sites/articles/archive/2013/0 8/15/emotional-pain-recovery-tips.aspx

According to, Dr. Steven Stosny wrote,

"Dwelling on the possible causes of emotional pain is more likely to exacerbate than ameliorate it. This is especially true when the hidden purpose of examining the possible causes is to assign blame.

To justify blame, we tend to magnify pain. Attributing blame then stimulates <u>anger</u> to punish the perceived offender. Biologically, the association of pain/vulnerability with anger is almost irresistible; anger has survival-based analgesic and <u>amphetamine</u> effects – it temporarily numbs pain and provides a surge of energy and <u>confidence</u> to ward-off threat. But each repetition of this process reinforces perceived damage and vulnerability by making defense seem more necessary.

Over time, the blame-anger response congeals into chronic resentment, which is a generalized, automatic defensive system geared to protect an ego made fragile by the perceived need for protection. To the resentful, painful emotions are not motivations to heal and improve but punishments inflicted by an unfair world. They try to control what other people think by devaluing or coercing them, thereby reinforcing the vulnerability they seek to avoid."

The Illusion of Control: Looking for It in All the Wrong Places

"Consider how little control we have over the things that most profoundly influence our lives. How many of us got to choose our parents? Did we decide the illnesses, accidents, medications, and substance use of our mothers during pregnancy? Who decided where and when they were born, how much money their families would have, what early childhood sickness or accidents they would experience, which schools they would go to and what kind of teachers and friends they would find there? Who chose whether other children would like or bully them, support or antagonize them, respect or humiliate them?"

Controlling the Meaning of Your Life

"You cannot control most of the major influences on your life, but you have absolute control over what they mean to you. If you control the meaning of events in your life by creating as much value as you can, you will have a sense of purpose and personal power. If you control it by devaluing yourself or others, you create a chronic sense of powerlessness, characterized by roller-coaster rides of adrenalin-driven resentment that crash into depressed moods. Rather than focus on the possible causes of pain and vulnerability, try to sort out what each hurtful incident means to you and what you can do to heal and improve. But do this important assessment with <u>self-compassion</u>, not self-criticism. Preoccupation with the causes of emotional pain tends to push us deeper into pain and bitterness; interpreting its meaning reveals <u>motivation</u> to heal and improve and moves us toward a brighter future."

Meaning vs. Expression

"Expressing negative emotions, without changing the meaning you give them, merely exercises them. Exercise sometimes produces exhaustion, but exhaustion never equals resolution or healing. Worse, expressing emotions repeatedly habituates them. "Crying the same blues over and over" creates more than monotony. It causes habitual sequences of <u>neural</u> firing that lead to repetitive, seemingly automatic behavior, such as having the same fight with your loved one over and over. If you find that you repeatedly make the same mistake or the same kinds of mistakes, you probably express negative emotions (or stuff them) without altering the meaning you give them, i.e., without focusing on healing and improving.

Some people are fortunate enough to resist the preoccupation with blame that characterizes the age of entitlement. But even for those lucky few, the search for causes of emotional pain has little chance of alleviating it. The causes of distressed conditions, which are usually complex interactions of many variables, are not often the same things that maintain them. Focusing on possible causes is more likely to make you feel damaged and vulnerable than lead to corrective or beneficial action."

Steven Stosny, Ph.D., is the founder of Compassion Power in suburban Washington, DC. Dr. Steven Stosny's most recent books are *Empowered Love* and *Soar Above: How to Use the Most Profound Part of Your Brain under Any Kind of Stress.* He has appeared on "The Oprah Winfrey Show," "The Today Show," "CBS Sunday Morning," and CNN's "Talkback Live" and "Anderson Cooper 360" and has been the subject of articles in, *The*

New York Times, *The Washington Post*, *U.S. News & World Report*, *The Wall Street Journal*, *Esquire*, *Cosmopolitan*, *O*, *Psychology Today*, *AP*, *Reuters*, and *USA Today*.
https://www.psychologytoday.com/us/blog/anger-in-the-age-entitlement/201107/the-meaning-emotional-pain

REFLECTION & NOTES

Love Beyond Pains Soul Verses

You must keep scriptures concerning your soul before your eyes.

Remember, your soul is your intellect, will, and emotions. The soul is God's design for you to feel His presence and to reason within your own mind your connection and relationship towards Him.

This is your free will as being human, making choices how you will live in this life. Losing your soul is equivalent to losing your mind. A double minded man is unstable in all his ways" (James 1:18).

There is no confusion where there is God's love. Perfect love, and there is only one perfect; cast out fear, fear has torment, (to the soul) he that fears is not made perfect in Christ love.

But if from there you seek the Lord your God, you will find him if you seek him with all your heart and with all your soul.

Deuteronomy 4:29 | NIV

What good will it be for someone to gain the whole world, yet forfeit their soul? Or what can anyone give in exchange for their soul?

Matthew 16:26 | NIV

Truly my soul finds rest in God; my salvation comes from him.

Psalm 62:1 | NIV

This is what the Lord says:
Stand at the crossroads and look;
ask for the ancient paths,
ask where the good way is, and walk
in it, and you will find rest for your
souls. But you said, 'We will not
walk in it.'

Jeremiah 6:16 | NIV

Why, my soul, are you downcast?
Why so disturbed within me?
Put your hope in God, for I will yet
praise him, my Savior and my God.

Psalm 42:11 | NIV

Jesus replied: 'Love the Lord your
God with all your heart and with all
your soul and with all your mind.'

Matthew 22:37 | NIV

Dear friend, I pray that you may

enjoy good health and that all may go well with you, even as your soul is getting along well.

3 John 1:2 | NIV

For you created my inmost being; you knit me together in my mother's womb. I praise you because I am fearfully and wonderfully made; your works are wonderful, I know that full well.

Psalm 139:13-14 | NIV

You will seek me and find me when you seek me with all your heart.

Jeremiah 29:13 | NIV

You, God, are my God, earnestly I seek you; I thirst for you, my whole being longs for you, in a dry and parched land where there is no water.

Psalm 63:1 | NIV

Praise the Lord, my soul; all my inmost being, praise his holy name.

Psalm 103:1 | NIV

Gracious words are a honeycomb, sweet to the soul and healing to the bones.

Proverbs 16:24 | NIV

I wait for the Lord, my whole being waits, and in his word I put my hope.

Psalm 130:5 | NIV

Save me, Lord, from lying lips and from deceitful tongues.

Psalm 120:2 | NIV

But be very careful to keep the commandment and the law that Moses the servant of the Lord gave you: to love the Lord your God, to walk in obedience to him, to keep his commands, to hold fast to him and to serve him with all your heart and with all your soul.

Joshua 22:5 | NIV

The law of the Lord is perfect, refreshing the soul.
The statutes of the Lord are trustworthy, making wise the simple.

Now I am about to go the way of all the earth. You know with all your heart and soul that not one of all the good promises the Lord your God gave you has failed. Every promise has been fulfilled; not one has failed.

Joshua 23:14 | NIV

My lips will shout for joy when I sing praise to you. I whom you have delivered.

Psalm 71:23 | NIV

Truly he is my rock and my salvation; he is my fortress, I will never be shaken.

Psalm 62:2 | NIV | 2/1/201

My lips will shout for joy when I sing praise to you. I whom you have delivered.

REFLECTION & NOTES

Conclusion

God Knows Us Better Than We Could Ever Know and Love Ourselves

In Matthew 10:30 states, "But the very hairs of your head are all numbered." That means those that are growing, have grown and will grow. God designed and created us as His workmanship. We know ourselves by what is known of us through Him. We love ourselves, by the love in which He loves us with and understand Him as being love. In this world we live in, people are murdered, rapes, abortion has rose. Individuals are cheated on, stole from, beaten and battered. So much damage is done to the soul and many die from the impact of it all. We were not designed to commit acts of hatred and crimes against one another. However, in the reality of our lives, it happens everywhere. We can only guard ourselves, be wise and protect those we love as much and as best we can. Soul wounds will not be avoided as long as you are human. The Apostle Paul, however, teaches us and admonishes us to live peaceable with all men. Not everyone gets this, and therefore as believers, we have to make quick decisions. Some can be avoided, some cannot, but remember you have the power to recover and love and live again and again. Choose the higher level of love as Christ did when he laid on the cross. Remember, he said, "Father forgive them for they know not what they are doing" Jesus understood our human condition was one of ignorance and weakness. When someone you love hurts your soul, forgive them. We hurt others' due to our humanism of ignorance and weaknesses. This is not an excuse for anyone to commit acts of crimes or sins or abuse of any sort against you. But, at least now, hopefully, you have a clear understanding of why they do it. Never, go back into a dangerous situation. Tell someone, get help and don't feel obligated to anyone that wants nothing but to cause you harm and pain. You owe them nothing, but to love and forgive them. The Bible tells us, OWE NO MAN NOTHING< BUT TO LOVE HIM!

The following quotes are from what I'd like to think are inspired by God. I was on the plane in November 2018 heading back from West Africa, Nigeria after a very exciting time of vacation that turned into my wedding. My flight was long, and I wasn't sleepy, so I wrote these quotes down until I felt the Spirit of God lift from me. I hope they become a blessing to your souls.

LOVE..... IS

Love is rare, there's nothing ordinary about it.

Love is a state of being, whatever is good, lovely, honest and pure that's love.

Love is costly, no expense should be spared.

Love is progressive, it's always moving forward, and it never retreats.

Loving is risky and pain maybe come, but turning something hurtful into something beautiful is still love.

Love is never blind, it sees all things from a clear unobstructed view in all directions. Emotions are blinding.

Love is not an emotion, it's an ignitor of our human condition that is innately emotional and built in.

Love is fueled by what is good.

Love is the hinge from which all other fruit of the spirit swings. You cannot have one without the other or claim too.

Love is truth, it knows no lie, nor can follow or create one.

Love is light, no darkness, sickness, death, or corruption can ever be found in it.

Love is waking up on a warm spring morning still finding dew glistening on the grass, flowers, and leaves.

Love is the juice that causes everything to grow.

Love has no ugly faces or unkind words, to do so would be equivalent to suicide. But even that is impossible for love.

Love doesn't figure out how to understand a matter. Wisdom and understanding are its compass and guide.

Love adjust and readjust without ever changing what it is. It only seeks to accommodate the user of it.

Love never imposes its will or seeks its own way. It is the way; the truth and your light follow it.

Love can ignite a person to become indisposed when it's inconvenient to do so. It leaves the individual to decide.

Love pushes pass pain because the gains have so much more dividends.

Love always wins, even when we think it loses.

Love can never be something that it's not. If we follow love's lead, we are forced to admit neither can we.

Love cannot be hypocritical, it would only contradict itself.

There's nothing fake or fantasy about love, it is what it is, nothing more, nothing less.

Love can never be altered, for God is love, and He changes not.

Love is the creator and life of all things seen and unseen.

Love does not have to take center stage to prove anything to anyone.

Love does not take, but it consistently and constantly gives out.

Love is an action word, forever doing great and mighty things.

Love is creative, its' designs are limitless.

Perfect love cast out anything and anyone that continues to fear and lives in darkness, it cannot.

Love is never confused or in doubt. Its' confidence is far from knowing.

Faith hope and love cannot operate without each other and will never go against one another.

Love does not have to test what it already knows.

Love will not place upon you that which it knows you cannot bear.

There are no tricks to love, it's strong and straight forward it needs no strings to puppet you along.

Love never leaves you wondering or questioning what happened.

Love guides you to all truth and knowledge, then comforts you.

Love has nothing to hide or a need to disguise itself.

There is no fear of retribution, resentment, discontent, or retaliation in love.

Love is pure and simple; to complicate it is to go against its grain into falsity.

Love is not hard to figure out, it's absolute.

Love is not proud or boastful.

Love is never torn between two opinions. It already has a permanent expectation and acceptance.

Love is not up one day, and down the next, we are.

Love gives, and never gets tired of giving.

Love is never at a loss; its pathway is always straight.

We are not centered around love, love encompasses us.

Love will never deny you.

Love pushes you forward and encourages you with the hopes and dreams it already knows is inside you.

Love empowers you with the strength of itself within you.

When someone says, "I LOVE YOU" love response is, DO YOU KNOW WHAT LOVE IS & WHAT YOU ARE SAYING?

Love is committed to all things love.

Love says, "I WILL, NOT I DO."

If we stop to inhale some of the things set forth here as to what in my opinion is love, getting passed pain, hurt, betrayal, disappointments, and unforgiveness will be like taking the ultimate pain reliever. No number of drugs or alcohol can heal you from emotional traumas, only His unfailing love.

Love Beyond Pain, so you can live again. You can walk & run while feeling wounds to your soul.

Thank You

Love Tommi

Inspiration is loves' best friend, and wisdom is its brother

984-209-0801

lovebeyondpains@gmail.com

website: http://bit.ly/lovebeyondpain